A FalconGuide® to the San Juan Islands

Help Us Keep This Guide Up to Date

Every effort has been made by the author and editors to make this guide as accurate and useful as possible. However, many things can change after a guide is published—establishments close, phone numbers change, hiking trails are rerouted, facilities come under new management, etc.

We would love to hear from you concerning your experiences with this guide and how you feel it could be improved and kept up to date. While we may not be able to respond to all comments and suggestions, we'll take them to heart and we'll also make certain to share them with the author. Please send your comments and suggestions to the following address:

The Globe Pequot Press
Reader Response/Editorial Department
P.O. Box 480
Guilford, CT 06437

Or you may e-mail us at:

editorial@GlobePequot.com

Thanks for your input, and happy trails!

Exploring Series

A FalconGuide® to the San Juan Islands

A Guide to Exploring the Great Outdoors

Dave Wortman

FALCON®

GUILFORD, CONNECTICUT
HELENA, MONTANA
AN IMPRINT OF THE GLOBE PEQUOT PRESS

A FALCON GUIDE®

Photo credits: pp. 25 and 170: Washington State Parks and Recreation Commission; p. 102: Erik Forssen; p. 106: Alan Jennings; p. 130: Matthew B. Ragen; p. 165: Bicycle Adventures; p. 167: Saul Kinderis. All other interior photos by the author.
Maps by David Sami, Multi Mapping LTD. © The Globe Pequot Press

ISSN 1553-1112
ISBN 0-7627-3107-9

Manufactured in the United States of America
First Edition/First Printing

To buy books in quantity for corporate use or incentives, call **(800) 962–0973, ext. 4551,** or e-mail **premiums@GlobePequot.com.**

*This book is dedicated to my late father, Sterling Wortman,
and to Ruth Wortman, my mother, whose strength and optimism
in the face of adversity never ceases to inspire me.*

San Juan park camping - Beach

Contents

Acknowledgments

I feel truly fortunate to have had the opportunity to explore and write about such a magical place as the San Juan Islands, and I have many people to thank for helping me on my journey. I would like to acknowledge my friends, particularly Lori Seabright and Alan Jennings, who offered company on several of my trips to the San Juans and lent their support along the way. I would also like to acknowledge the tremendous support I received from Deborah Hopkins and Robin Jacobson of the San Juan Islands Visitors Bureau, who provided information resources, helped me check facts, and connected me with people throughout the islands. Last but certainly not least, I owe my gratitude to the many park managers, guides, charter operators, community leaders, and caring residents throughout the islands. They shared with me their knowledge of and love for the San Juans in many ways, whether it was providing their expertise about plants and wildlife, allowing me to join them on a trip, or offering their input to draft chapters.

Introducing the San Juan Islands

What best defines Washington's San Juan Islands? Perhaps it's the deep green forests that cover their hills and mountainsides and invite exploration. Or maybe it's their emerald bays and quiet coves that shelter colorful tide pools, abundant bird life, and playful marine mammals. Others would say it's their rolling farmland and quiet rural countryside, where life just seems a little simpler. No matter how you choose to define them, there's little doubt that the San Juans are a special place. You can gently skim across calm blue waters on an early morning paddle, feel the crunch of pebbles underfoot walking on your favorite beach, or watch the golden sunset from a forested bluff. What's perhaps most amazing of all is how close it all is to the sprawling bustle of Seattle and Vancouver, yet how far removed it all feels.

Washington State is well known for its outdoor recreation opportunities, and the San Juan Islands are certainly no exception. The hundreds of miles of shoreline, narrow passages, coves, bays, and straits provide some of the best sea kayaking in the country. Cyclists flock to the islands to enjoy the miles of quiet rural roads, while hikers will find walks of all levels to open summits, through quiet forests, and along beautiful beaches and shorelines. The islands are also a top destination for whale watching, boating, diving, fishing, and other outdoor pursuits.

But make no mistake: The San Juans have definitely been discovered. Tourism is now the leading industry in the islands, long ago outpacing the mainstays of farming, fishing, and forestry. Tourism has been both a blessing to the economy of the islands and a challenge to their traditional way of life. Over the last twenty years, the popularity of the San Juans has soared, bringing with it wealthy film stars and retirees, escalating real estate values, longer ferry lines, and increasingly strained tourist amenities. Once uncommon, NO TRESPASSING signs have sprung up around the islands, a sign of the increasing conflict between residents and visitors. And many more are coming here to stay too—the population of the San Juans grew more than 40 percent in the 1990s and continues to increase.

There is a bright side to all of the popularity. The rapid change has sparked an active preservation movement, and thanks to some far-sighted individuals, you'll find much of the "old life" preserved on the islands, from shorelines to historic farms. Still largely free from big-box development and corporate retail chains, a warm, small-town feel still greets visitors in places like Friday Harbor

The San Juan Islands

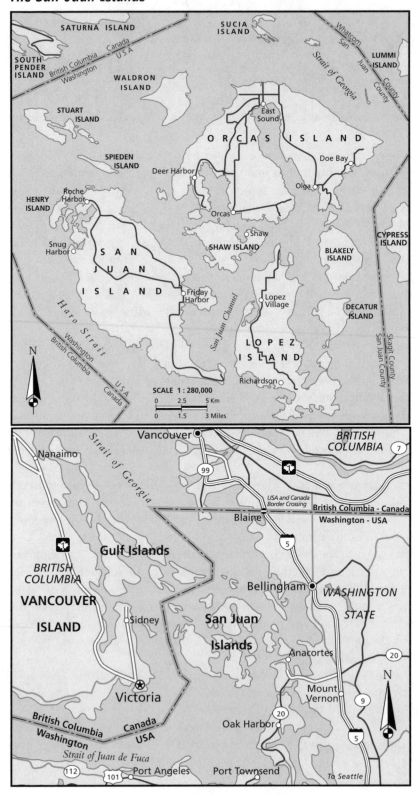

and East Sound. Several federal, state, and local parks protect islands, bays, and wildlife habitat, also providing for public access and enjoyment. And unlike twenty years ago, today's visitor will find an extensive choice in amenities, particularly those related to the outdoors, including guided kayak trips and nature walks, bike shops, sailing cruises, diving excursions, and rental stores that provide everything for the novice and expert alike.

Defining the Islands

There's little agreement about how best to geographically define the San Juans, let alone how many islands there are in the archipelago. Straddling the U.S./Canada border, many local residents and ecologists put the San Juans in the center of the "Salish Sea,"—including Puget Sound, Canada's Strait of Georgia, and the Strait of Juan de Fuca—to recognize the greater ecological, cultural, and geographical region.

During the lowest tides there may be more than 780 distinct "islands" visible in the San Juans, some no more than a small outcrop, but only 175 of these are large enough to have names. And while 30 of these larger islands are inhabited by a year-round population of about 15,000, most residents live on the four main islands served by the ferry system: Lopez, Orcas, San Juan, and Shaw. Not surprisingly, these are also the islands where visitors will find the most amenities and many of the outdoor recreation opportunities.

Each of the main islands has developed not only a distinct character but also dedicated followings of both residents and visitors. When it comes to outdoor recreation, one reason may be that the distinct conditions on each island draw people seeking different outdoor pursuits—Lopez is famous for its biking terrain, Orcas for its hiking trails, and San Juan for its recreational whale-watching and kayaking opportunities.

Orcas, the largest of the three islands at 58 square miles, is by far the most rugged and forested, dominated by Moran State Park and the slopes of Mount Constitution, rising over 2,400 feet above the island. The park not only makes a good base for campers exploring the island, it's also full of hiking and biking options, from easy lakeshore strolls to grinding climbs providing spectacular views from Mount Constitution's open summit. Kayakers also find Orcas a good jumping-off point for exploring many of the smaller state marine park islands in the region. Among its approximately 4,500 residents, you'll find an eclectic community of farmers, artists, fishermen, retirees, writers, and weekend vacationers. East Sound, located near the center of the horseshoe-shaped island, is the hub of activity and the home of most of the island's shops and services. Smaller communities include Olga, Deer Harbor, Orcas Landing, and West Sound.

San Juan Island, the most populated with nearly 7,000 people, is perhaps the best known of the San Juans, with an abundance of culture, history, scenery, and

Land Preservation

As the San Juan Islands have grown in popularity, so too have the pressures to develop them. For the last thirty years, the population of San Juan County has been one of the fastest growing in Washington. The development has not only threatened the scenic beauty of the islands, it's also put a serious strain on the water supply and environment.

Luckily, the islands are also home to a strong land preservation movement. It's one that has successfully protected thousands of acres from development and provided valuable public access to shorelines. Yet with spiraling real estate prices, the work is far from over. Here are a few of the groups working to protect the San Juan Islands :

- The San Juan County Land Bank (360–378–4402, www.co.san-juan.wa.us/land_bank) purchases land outright and conservation easements on private land using tax revenue from real estate transactions. As of 2001 the Land Bank had protected about 2,500 acres.

- The nonprofit San Juan Preservation Trust (360–468–3202, www.sjpt.org) is supported by 1,500 members and has protected more than 8,900 acres in the islands.

- The Nature Conservancy (206–343–4344, nature.org/wherewework/north america/states/washington), the nation's largest land conservation organization, has purchased and manages several key properties throughout the islands, including Yellow Island in the Wasp Islands group, Sentinel Island just south of Spieden Island, and Goose Island off the tip of San Juan Island.

- The nonprofit Friends of the San Juans (360–378–2319, www.sanjuans.org) works on a variety of programs, from urban growth to marine habitat preservation.

To do your part in preserving the islands, you can support such groups and tread lightly during your visit by conserving water, staying on trails, and properly disposing of litter. Some preservation-minded folks are also opting out of building their own vacation homes in the islands, taking advantage of the many wonderful lodges, hotels, cabins, and vacation homes for rent throughout the San Juans.

nature. Hikers will find plenty of options in the two units of the San Juan Island National Historical Park, and kayakers will be tempted to explore the island's many bays and rugged shorelines. It's also the most developed of the islands, where you'll find icons of old island life mixed with the new. Slightly smaller

Ferry leaving Friday Harbor, San Juan Island

than Orcas at about 14.5 miles long and 6.5 miles wide, San Juan Island is home to an active farming community, rolling forested hills, and quiet bays that can all be explored by bike in a day or two. Friday Harbor, the island's hub and the largest town in the San Juans with a population of 2,000, is a bustling port that has managed to maintain its historic charm, with lots of lodging opportunities, pubs and restaurants, and a scenic waterfront. Fertile glacial valleys in the center of the island support farms, while two ranges of hills—Mount Dallas and the San Juan ranges—form forested, hilly backdrops along the west side of the island.

Lopez, named after the Spanish explorer Lopez Gonzalez de Haro, is the least developed of the four major islands and is considerably smaller at just over 29 square miles. It's a scenic patchwork of farmland, interspersed with forest and some spectacular coastline, particularly on the south side of the island. By 1930 Lopez was well established as the largest farming community in the San Juans, with over 130 farms producing everything from cattle to fruits and vegetables. While many of the island's large farms have been sold off, visitors will find that Lopez still has a thriving farm community growing a variety of organic produce and livestock. It's not only the driest of the major islands, it's also the most level, with a high point of only 480 feet, which draws cyclists to its pastoral landscape. Its population also shares a strong environmental ethic and values a quieter way of life. You're also likely to get the trademark "Lopez wave" as you drive, walk, or cycle past its friendly residents.

Surrounded by the three other large islands, Shaw Island lies at the geographic center of the San Juans. It's also the smallest of the four major islands at only 7.7 square miles and is home to just over 200 residents. Until 2004 Shaw's best-known residents were its Franciscan nuns, who for more than twenty years regularly ran the island's ferry docks and owned the only store on the island. (Today a Shaw Island family operates the docks and the store.) Visitors will find no restaurants or overnight accommodations on Shaw, but those wanting a quiet escape here will find lonely roads for cycling, quiet shorelines for paddling, and a scenic beachfront campground.

Island History

The San Juans that visitors experience today, including their place names and history, are the product of a rich cultural past. In fact, human visitation to the islands dates back thousands of years. Long before the arrival of Spanish, British, and U.S. explorers in the 1700s and 1800s, the region's Native Americans, often referred to as the Coast Salish, regularly visited the islands for fishing and shellfishing—over time, some came to live here too. These earliest native visitors and residents shared language and religious beliefs with the native peoples on present-day Vancouver Island to the north in Canada and on mainland Washington and British Columbia, including the Saanich, Lummi, Songhees, and Samish tribes.

Coast Salish inhabitation of the San Juans may in fact date back more than 11,500 years. It is believed that the Coast Salish first visited the San Juans during summers, coming from the mainland to hunt deer and other game, fish for salmon, harvest clams, and dig camas flower bulbs. About 4,000 years ago great forests of cedar trees started to appear on the islands, allowing the Salish to build plank houses and canoes and to weave clothing from the trees' stringy bark. Over time, as they discovered ways to store food, the Coast Salish started to move to the islands about 1,500 years ago. Arts flourished during this time as they made carvings, weavings, and tools that are today's rich cultural symbols of their past.

Many Coast Salish in the San Juans had strong connections to the sea, living on diets of cockles, mussels, oysters, sea cucumbers, snails, barnacles, and urchins harvested from mudflats and rocky shorelines. Crabs were speared from canoes, and clams harvested with digging sticks and eaten raw or steamed over fires. The Coast Salish were also adept at reef netting, a technique that involved draping a net between two canoes or a land point and a canoe to catch salmon, one of the mainstays in their diet. Harvested fish were often filleted and dried on racks. The Salish also built plank houses for various facets of everyday life,

Old homestead and madrone trees, Shaw Island

from storing food to sleeping, eating, and conducting ceremonies. Yet even with all of this knowledge, archaeologists are only beginning to understand the true richness of Salish life in the islands, as only a few of the undoubtedly hundreds of archaeological sites throughout the San Juans have been thoroughly investigated.

Like much of the rest of North America, change was inevitable in the San Juans with the arrival of European and, eventually, American explorers. In the late 1590s, Juan de Fuca, the Greek explorer to whom the Strait of Juan de Fuca owes its name, sailed along the Northwest coast and mistakenly claimed to have found a long-sought-after Northwest passage from the Pacific Ocean to the east. Spanish explorers sailed to the Pacific Northwest in the late 1700s, finally reaching the San Juans in 1791, marked by the arrival of explorers Lopez Gonzales de Haro and Francisco Eliza. A year later they were joined by English explorer George Vancouver and his survey crew, who landed at Blind Bay on today's Shaw Island.

Americans would not make it to the San Juans until fifty years later in 1841, but their eventual arrival set the stage for the transformation of the islands by white settlers. The first non-native settlers of the San Juans were members of the Hudson's Bay Company, who came to the islands between 1813 and 1853 to hunt and trade furs. Among these were, interestingly, many seafaring Hawaiians who left their tropical islands to join the company's fur trade as seamen and stevedores. They called themselves *kanakas*, a word that came to mean Hawaiian in the Pacific Northwest. They settled on Canada's Vancouver and Salt Spring Islands, and on the south side of San Juan Island, the site of today's Kanaka Bay. A Hawaiian named Joe Poalie, better known locally as "Joe Friday," settled on San Juan Island in the 1850s; he lived on the east side of the island near the water, grazing sheep near what now is Friday Harbor.

Soon after, the British and Americans established more posts on the islands for fur trading. As interest in the islands among the Americans and British grew, so too did their tensions over possession of the islands. The conflict peaked with the "Pig War" on San Juan Island; the joint British-American occupation of San Juan Island was finally resolved in 1872 when the island was awarded to the United States by the German arbiter Kaiser Wilhelm.

As more settlers discovered the islands in the 1800s, the San Juans developed a bustling economy built on farming, forestry, and fishing. Orcas Island supported a healthy fruit-farming community during this time, and in the peak season about 160,000 boxes of apples per year were shipped out of East Sound, bound for the mainland. Olga, West Sound, and Deer Harbor also served as shipping hubs on the island. Fruit was also grown to a lesser extent on other islands. On San Juan Island, farming, fishing, two lime quarries, yachting, and government administration formed a diverse economy during the 1800s. Friday Harbor, the seat of present-day San Juan County, was first recognized as a town in 1877.

With all of their prosperity, the San Juans also have a darker side to their history. Smugglers transporting both goods and people from Canada to the United States found the many bays and coves in the islands both convenient refuge and a good place to do business. During prohibition alcohol smugglers often visited the San Juans to drop their shipments, sometimes sparking hijackings or violence. Even to this day, Coast Guard border patrols throughout the islands remain vigilant for illegal trafficking between the two countries.

Population growth continued on the islands in the 1900s, with farming and fishing, along with forestry, contributing to economic growth. While visitors in the early 1900s could come to the San Juans as foot passengers, it was not until the 1930s that the first auto ferry started servicing the islands, opening them up to the tourism and recreation that is such an important part of island life today.

Flora and Fauna

For such a small geographic area, the San Juans contain an amazing diversity of vegetation types, ranging from thick, moist forests to dry grasslands. These differences owe their existence to not only the varied topography and climate in the islands, but also the changes introduced by humans over the years.

Perhaps most characteristic of the islands are their lush, green coniferous forests. While much of the forest on the San Juans was cleared for farming or harvested for timber in the mid-1800s, many of these areas have grown back in dense second-growth stands, particularly on Orcas and San Juan Islands. With some trees reaching 300 to 400 years old, majestic forests still grow in places like the south end of Lopez Island, parts of Moran State Park on Orcas Island, and American Camp on San Juan Island. Species typical of moist forests in the San Juans include Douglas fir, western red cedar, and western hemlock. Sitka spruce can be found in moist valleys, while other areas support grand fir, red alder, and bigleaf maple.

In stark contrast to dense forests, grassy meadows and balds thrive in drier areas and on rocky ridges throughout the San Juan Islands, including places like the west side of San Juan Island, the south side of Lopez Island, and on south-facing hillsides on Orcas Island. These areas support stands of Garry oak and Rocky Mountain juniper, along with the beautiful Pacific madrone. On Orcas Island's Mount Constitution, you'll find one of western Washington's largest stands of lodgepole pine. Flowers found in the islands include buttercup, chocolate lily, shooting star, blue camas, and Calypso orchid. Washington's only native cactus species, the prickly pear cactus, is found on drier sites throughout the islands.

The varied habitats of the San Juans support many different species of wildlife—some native, others introduced throughout island history. The large-scale clearing of forests on the islands 150 years ago, combined with hunting, eliminated bigger land mammals such as bear and elk, along with several bird species. While the large mammals did not return, several bird species like pileated woodpecker, Cooper's hawk, and owls have made a comeback. Today you'll find an abundance of birds and small mammals, and deer are notoriously tame in the islands—so much so that it's not uncommon to find them eager to eat out of your hand (although this is highly discouraged). Non-native species you might be surprised to find in the San Juans, some of which were brought to the islands for sport hunting, include red fox, wild turkey, ring-necked pheasant, and California quail. European rabbits, also non-native, are common on Lopez Island and parts of San Juan Island, identified by their trademark extensive networks of warrens (dens).

The marine environment around the 400 miles of coastline in the San Juan Islands is among the richest in the world, including straits more than 1,000 feet deep, shallow bays, rocky islets and coastlines, sand and pebble beaches, and mudflats. Strong tidal currents common throughout the region continually flush large volumes of water through the straits around the San Juans, a result of the

Bald eagles, San Juan Islands

twice-daily intertidal exchange between the Strait of Juan de Fuca and the Strait of Georgia. This dynamic flux produces a mixing of cold, salty ocean waters with brackish surface waters. Currents force waters from deep channels upward over submerged ridges, creating an exchange of oxygen and nutrients, also fed by

Preserving the Marine Environment

The Transborder Marine Protected Area (MPA) Initiative is a joint project sponsored by San Juan County and nongovernment organizations. Its goal is to increase public awareness of the state of the marine resources in the Salish Sea and to protect and sustain them by designating a network of marine protected areas between San Juan County and the Canadian Gulf Islands.

Supporters note that far from being separate and isolated, the waters between the United States and Canada are a single ecosystem being affected by habitat disruption and pollution from both north and south of the border. Orca whale populations and stocks of fisheries for many species are declining sharply, and increasing shipping activity in Haro Strait, Boundary Pass, and Rosario Strait is heightening the risk of fuel and chemical spills and the introduction of invasive non-native species. Industrial pollutants discharged to the region's waters from mainland sources end up in the food chain of fish, marine mammals, and seabirds.

The MPA Initiative is pushing for the establishment of a network of marine preserve areas to protect productive ecosystems and biological diversity, conserve fisheries resources, and promote scientific research. For more information contact the San Juan County Marine Resources Committee (360–378–1095, www.sjcmrc.org).

nutrients from streams and rivers. Marine mammals inhabiting these productive waters include California sea lions, humpback whales, gray whales, orca whales, minke whales, Dall's porpoises, Pacific white-sided porpoises, harbor porpoises, harbor seals, Steller's sea lions, elephant seals, and river otters. Offshore banks, reefs, and shelves along the continental coastline of the San Juans also feature luxuriant forests of bull kelp. Eelgrass beds, found in shallow bays, are highly productive areas supporting rich flora, marine animals, birds, and bottom fish and serving as refuge for migrating juvenile salmon and forage fish.

More than 290 species of birds have been observed in the San Juan Islands. In open-water areas, tide rips, kelp reefs, bays, and eelgrass beds support loons, grebes, murres, murrelets, mergansers, harlequin ducks, gulls, terns, and alcids. Along rocky shorelines and on offshore rocks, you can spot black oystercatchers, killdeer, and rock sandpipers, as well as three species of cormorants, pigeon guillemots, and tufted puffins. Hundreds of rhinoceros auklets also come to San Juan Channel every summer to forage, while in the fall and early winter, several bird species join harbor seals as they prey on schools of herring in the numerous bays around the islands. The distinctive chattering call of the blue-and-white kingfisher is a familiar sound around the shorelines, as is the sight of the prehistoric-looking great blue heron, often seen foraging in shallows or perched in waterside treetops. The San Juans also support one of the largest bald-eagle populations in the United States—eagles are found both nesting in tall conifer trees near the shoreline and foraging over waters for salmon and other fish.

Island Geology

The topography and geology of the San Juans reflect quite a complex and sometimes baffling geologic history. The immense diversity in rock content and formations you'll see as you travel around the islands includes marine fossils in places like the Sucia Islands, granite outcrops on the slopes of Mount Constitution on Orcas Island, pillow basalts on the south side of Lopez Island and the west side of San Juan Island, and limestone on the north side of San Juan Island. Geologists believe that like a giant tossed salad, rapid burial and uplift of the various geologic units helped juxtapose already-formed "terranes," or geologically distinct formations, into the jumbled arrangement found in the islands today.

Looking at the big picture, the San Juans are made up of an assemblage of rocks laid down in a large ocean trench, then uplifted by tectonic forces. The islands are part of a small plate that rides on top of a denser Pacific oceanic plate, itself sliding under the lighter continental North American plate to the east. The force of impact from these colliding plates has forced the San Juan Islands upward, creating a series of faults across the islands, mixing and metamorphosing rocks in the process. Many of the original sedimentary and volcanic rocks of the San Juans have been transformed into metamorphic rocks, while others remain in their original state.

Although there are disagreements on exactly how to categorize the geologically complex islands, geologists generally divide the San Juans into several distinct terranes. The San Juan terrane, covering San Juan Island, Shaw Island, and most of Orcas Island, is the most complex, consisting of limestone accumulated in shallow water, mudstone and chert on the deep ocean floor, and scraps of oceanic crust. What you'll see at the surface today is a mixture composed of these underlying rocks, overlain in some areas by glacial deposits. For example, parts of English Camp on San Juan Island are covered with Middle to Upper Paleozoic sedimentary and volcanic rocks, while other areas of the island are covered with Jurassic-Cretaceous sedimentary and volcanic rocks.

The Decatur Formation, consisting mostly of rocks from about 150 million years ago, covers most of Cypress Island, Decatur Island, Clark Island, Obstruction Island, the north half of Lopez Island, and the tip of Orcas Island. It consists mainly of thick sections of sandstone and pebble conglomerates

East Point near village of East Sound, Orcas Island

along with slabs of ocean crust. The Lopez Formation, covering the south half of Lopez Island, also consists of rocks about 150 million years old, mainly sedimentary rocks from the deep ocean floor. Deformation and heating have turned many of these rocks into dark slates. Finally, the much younger Nanaimo Formation shows up only in the far northwest corner of the San Juans. Made up of much less deformed oceanic sediments, it covers the north tip of Orcas, Waldron, Stuart, Sucia, Patos, and Matia Islands.

The San Juan Islands were also directly in the path of Pleistocene glaciers that formed in and advanced south from the mountains of western British Columbia. The Fraser glaciation, which occurred from about 10,000 to 18,500 years ago, was the last period of glaciation to affect the San Juans, and its influences are readily visible today. Glacial ice over a mile thick in places covered the islands, and the powerful eroding force of the glaciers scraped, smoothed, and rounded their landscape, gouging out channels such as Haro Strait to depths of nearly 1,300 feet, while the islands, composed of harder rock, remained more intact. Glacial striations, consisting of grooves scraped in the bedrock, also tell the tale of these glacial processes, particularly on the slopes and summits of Mount Constitution, its summit over 3,700 feet higher than the bottom of Haro Strait.

As the Fraser glacier melted and retreated, it deposited materials around the San Juan Islands. Mount Finlayson and the bluffs along South Beach on the southern part of San Juan Island is one such depositional area, a glacial moraine comprising outwash sands and clays. The moraine along South Beach directly below Cattle Point Road varies in height from 30 to 100 feet. Glacial erratics, which include rocks and boulders deposited as glaciers melted, are also visible in parts of American Camp.

Island Weather

Among all of the great qualities of Washington and the San Juan Islands, few would list the weather as the region's largest selling point. True, the climate in the San Juans can be dark and dreary at times, but think twice if you're ready to write off a trip to the islands because of their weather.

In western Washington, topography plays a big role in making weather. The San Juan Islands lie in the rain shadow of the Olympic Mountains to the southwest. As moisture-laden air sweeps in from the southwest off the Pacific Ocean, it runs up against the Olympic Mountains, where it is forced to rise, wringing out most of its moisture. Under these conditions, it's no wonder that the south and west valleys of the Olympic Peninsula are the wettest places in the continental United States. But by the time these air masses reach the San Juans, much of their moisture has been left behind, meaning that the San Juans see a fraction of the rainfall—just 17 to 19 inches in a typical year. That's less than half the annual rainfall of Seattle. Rainfall can even vary in the San Juan Islands themselves, with less rain on the south end of Lopez Island, and more rain in the northern islands.

Not only is there less rainfall in the San Juans, it's also very seasonal. There's little wonder why summers in the San Juans are so popular. In addition to the long days, summers are sunny and pleasantly cool to warm, with high temperatures in the sixties and seventies—only occasionally do warm spells push temperatures into the eighties. Nights are cool, with lows in the fifties. July is typically the driest month, although periods of pleasant warm weather can extend all the way from May into mid-October. September and early October often bring clear autumn days and crisp nights. As air temperatures cool later in the summer and in early fall, fog may form around the islands, and while usually burning off by early afternoon, it may persist in some spots for much of the day.

Winter is a different story in the San Juans. Nearly 70 percent of the region's rain falls from October to April. November, December, and January are particularly rainy, and frequent winter storms can bring with them high winds as well. Temperatures are usually in the forties in late fall and winter, though occasional arctic fronts from the north bring with them snow, which usually lasts less than a day or so. The one exception is on Mount Constitution on Orcas Island, where, at nearly 2,500 feet, snows may accumulate for longer periods. But even in winter, periods of clear weather with brilliant sunny days regularly punctuate the gray skies, when stunning views of the snowcapped Olympic and Cascades Mountains can make a dramatically scenic backdrop.

The National Weather Service (www.wrh.noaa.gov) in Seattle issues regular weather updates for zones around western Washington, including the San Juans and surrounding area. The Weather Service also issues regular marine forecasts for northern inland waters of Washington, including the waters around the San Juan Islands. These forecasts include wind speed and direction as well as predicted wave heights. Regular marine-condition updates and forecasts from both Canada and the United States are also available by VHF radio, a helpful resource for boaters and kayakers to help anticipate upcoming weather conditions.

How to Use This Guide

The following chapters provide difficulty ratings for the various trips as guidance for people of varying fitness and skill levels. These are intended to be general guidelines, as each individual's capabilities will vary. For chapters 2 and 4, easy hikes or cycle trips are generally considered to be short in length, with minimal elevation gain on a well-graded trail or road surface. Moderate trips are of moderate length, with some steeper climbs and descents. Strenuous trips cover longer distances, with significant grades and elevation gains. For paddle trips, easier trips include those in waters more protected from strong currents or exposure to winds, and where less-experienced paddlers can generally stay close to shore. Moderate trips include exposure to some currents and tide rips, more exposure to wind-driven seas, and/or short open-water crossings. Strenuous trips include significant exposure to currents, winds, and tide rips, with substantial open-water crossings. Even with these ratings, however, local conditions may vary widely based on daily weather and tides.

The maps throughout this book provide general information about hiking, cycling, and paddling routes. They are not intended to be a substitute for more detailed topographical maps or nautical charts. Readers are recommended to consult with park and resource managers to obtain more detailed maps and up-to-date information on route conditions before embarking on a trip.

Generally, permits are not required to hike, cycle, or paddle in the San Juan Islands. However, readers should be aware that other regulations do apply from area to area. In many parks and recreation areas, leashed pets are permitted, but they are typically prohibited in natural area preserves. Campfires are largely restricted to designated fire pits, and advanced reservations may be required to book a campsite. Because of the fragile nature and high use of many areas of the San Juans, visitors are also encouraged to stay on maintained trails, pack out garbage, use fresh water sparingly, observe wildlife from a safe distance, and leave plant life for others to enjoy. It's a good idea to contact park and resource managers to obtain the most up-to-date information on regulations, as they may change seasonally and from year to year.

Legend

———————	Major Road
═══════════	Secondary Road
———————	Other Road (paved or unpaved)
▪▪▪▪▪▪▪▪▪▪▪	Hiking Trail
- - - - - - -	Other Trail
- - - →- -	Kayak Route
/////////////	Park
⚘ ⚘	Wetlands
—·—·—·-	International Boundary
—··—··—	County Boundary
Λ	Campground
⊞	Day Recreation Area
⟆	Beach
Ⓟ	Parking
◻	Viewpoint
■	Structure
⦚	Falls
Ï	Lighthouse
•—•	Gate
🚶START	Trailhead
🚻	Restroom

When to Go

If you're wondering when to visit the San Juans, it's helpful to consider a few factors. In reality, their mild climate and easy accessibility make them an attractive place to visit at any time of year—in fact, many mainlanders living within a few hours of the ferry come for quick weekend getaways year-round. There are, however, some distinct tradeoffs between crowds and weather for each season that are worth considering.

The San Juan Islands are most popular between Memorial Day and Labor Day. July and August are typically the peak visitor months, when the weather is predictably warmer, and the days sunnier and longer. But while the weather may be the upside of a visit during summer, you'll also contend with more headaches too—long ferry lines, fully booked campgrounds, more boats on the water, and more company on the roads and trails. Prices are also generally higher for lodging during peak season. You can plan to beat at least some of the crowds by scheduling your trip during midweek.

May and September are especially pleasant months to visit the San Juan Islands—the crowds are smaller, the weather is regularly warm and sunny, and there are plenty of opportunities to cycle, hike, kayak, or watch wildlife. And even though most rain in the San Juans falls between October and April, a trip during this time of year deserves some serious consideration. Weather in the islands can be beautiful well into October, with sunny days and crisp fall nights. Even during the middle of winter, you'll rarely find snow in the San Juans, and the regular stretches of clear weather can be glorious. The off-season also offers the advantages of shorter ferry lines, open campgrounds, and lower lodging prices. Best of all, you're more likely to have a trail to hike or road to bike all to yourself. Even kayakers and boaters will find good off-season opportunities, although longer or more exposed trips need to be carefully considered given the shorter days, colder temperatures, and greater likelihood of rough weather.

Getting There

By far the most popular way to reach the San Juans is by the drive-on ferries operated by the Washington State ferry system. Ferries depart several times each day from the main ferry terminal located in Anacortes, about 85 miles north of Seattle. In fact, the state ferry is the only choice if you're planning to explore the San Juans in the freedom of your own car.

Loading the ferry, Orcas Island

Ferries from Anacortes sail to Lopez, Shaw, Orcas, and San Juan Islands, while some ferry runs also connect to Canada's Vancouver Island. If you're looking to explore among each of the larger islands once in the San Juans, Washington State Ferries also runs an interisland service, connecting the four larger islands with several trips each day. On all routes, be sure to specify which island you'd like to go to, as different routes serve different islands.

Whether you're riding from Anacortes to the San Juan Islands or on the ferry between the islands, the ferry ride is a highly scenic experience in itself, with sweeping views of mountains, straits, forested islands, and narrow passageways. It's not unusual to see seals, eagles, or even the occasional porpoise or whale from the ferry, along with abundant seabird life.

But there is a distinct downside to the public ferries. The surging popularity of the islands has made getting to them an increasingly challenging ordeal, particularly in summer. On summer weekends, waiting times for cars boarding at the Anacortes terminal can be in excess of two hours, and no advanced bookings are allowed. If you can, plan your departure during midweek when ferry lines are typically shorter and fees cheaper. Otherwise, come prepared to wait—a small handful of restaurants near the ferry terminal provide some options for distraction.

If you're willing to part with your car, heading to the islands on foot or with your bike is not only cheaper, but you can also avoid all of the hassles of long waits for drive-on traffic. If you're heading to Friday Harbor on San Juan Island, for example, there are many in-town lodging options within a few minutes' walk of the ferry terminal. Shuttle bus services or taxis are also available on Lopez, Orcas, and San Juan Islands, as are car rentals. And because of the islands' small size, most of their campgrounds and other destinations are easily reachable by bike. Kayaks on hand-carried trailers can also be walked onto ferries, though public launching opportunities at the island ferry landings are limited.

If you're planning to walk onto the ferry, you'll find parking at one of the several parking lots at the Anacortes ferry terminal. Fees apply in summer, but parking is free in the off-season. In peak season these lots too can fill up, particularly on weekends. Another option to consider is the free parking at the Skagit County park-and-ride alongside Highway 20 at South March's Point Road, just east of Anacortes, where you'll find a free shuttle to the ferry terminal. Those traveling by bus or train will find connections from Mount Vernon to the Anacortes ferry terminal.

Many private charter operators are taking advantage of the increasing frustrations with the state ferry and offering their own service to the islands. Charter boat services now run from Anacortes, Bellingham, and other nearby ports, offering transportation to and from Lopez, Orcas, and San Juan Islands, as well as travel to most of the smaller islands not served by the ferry system. You'll also find several flights to the San Juans from the mainland from as far away as Seattle and Portland, Oregon. San Juan, Orcas, and Lopez Islands all have small airports, and seaplane floats are available at San Juan Island's Friday Harbor and Roche Harbor.

Camping, Lodging, and Other Essentials

Many visitors coming to the San Juans to experience the outdoors choose to camp at one of the many sites throughout the islands. Camping choices range from the primitive to full-facility sites, and from small and intimate state and county parks to high-volume private campground resorts.

You'll find camping on all of the major islands served by the ferry—Lopez, Orcas, San Juan, and Shaw. Some sites are run by San Juan County Parks or Washington State Parks, while others are privately owned and operated. Still other camping options can be found on many of the smaller outer islands that are part of the state park system or are under other public ownership. Outer island camping is a particularly good option for those who are kayaking or boating throughout the islands. These destinations are also increasingly served by local charter boats.

No matter where you go, one word of caution: Like many other facilities, campsites in the San Juans are in high demand, and many are at capacity in

Travel Essentials

Ferry Information

- To get to the Anacortes ferry terminal from Seattle, drive north on Interstate 5, take exit 230, and drive west on Highway 20, following the Highway 20 Spur through Anacortes. Ferry directions are marked with signs.
- To view ferry waiting times, fares, and other information, go to www.wsdot .wa.gov/ferries, or call (800) 84–FERRY.
- See www.skat.org or call Skagit Transit at (360) 757–4433 for more information on parking, shuttles, and connecting buses to the ferry terminal.

By Air

- Kenmore Air (800–543–9595, www.kenmoreair.com) offers daily flights from Seattle's Lake Union to various destinations in the San Juan Islands and Canada.
- San Juan Airlines (800–874–4434, www.sanjuanairlines.com) flies between Seattle, Bellingham, Anacortes, Port Angeles, British Columbia, and the San Juan Islands.
- Northwest Seaplanes (800–690–0086, www.nwseaplanes.com) has flights to the San Juans from the south end of Lake Washington, just south of Seattle.
- West Isle Air (800–874–4434, www.westisleair.com) provides scheduled flights from Anacortes to the San Juan Islands.

By Private Charter Boat

- Paraclete Charters (800–808–2999, www.paracletecharters.com), based in Anacortes, provides transportation to custom destinations in the islands

summer. Fortunately for those willing to plan ahead, many campgrounds now allow you to book several months in advance, either by phone or via the Internet. With the exception of private campgrounds, most camping in the off-season is first-come, first served, and finding a site is usually much less of a problem past the Labor Day weekend.

The number of lodging options in the San Juans has multiplied over the last decade, and you'll now find a full range of choices, from simple cabins to top-end hotels and nationally recognized bed-and-breakfasts. Like camping, don't expect to come to the San Juans in summer and find any last-minute lodging—many places are fully booked during the peak summer season. The last thing any family needs is to arrive on one of the islands late at night only to be turned twenty-four hours a day, seven days a week. Special events and package tours are available, and both kayaks and bikes can be carried onboard. Fares are based on travel "zones" in the islands.

- Island Express (877–473–9777, www.islandexpresscharters.com) also runs trips between Anacortes and several locations in the San Juans. Fares are also based on travel "zones."
- Island Commuter (888–734–8180, www.islandcommuter.com) offers daily service between Bellingham and Friday Harbor.
- Victoria Express (360–452–8088, www.victoriaexpress.com) provides daily ferry service between Port Angeles and Friday Harbor.
- Victoria Clipper (800–888–2535, www.victoriaclipper.com) runs high-speed catamaran trips from Seattle to Friday Harbor.

On-Island Shuttles, Taxis, and Rental Cars

- San Juan Island Transit and Tours (800–887–8387, www.sanjuantransit.com) provides transport around San Juan Island, with shuttles between Friday Harbor and Roche Harbor.
- San Juan Taxi, San Juan Island, (360) 378–3550
- Bob's Taxi, San Juan Island, (877) TAXI–BOB
- A Lopez Cab, (360) 468–2227
- Orcas Island Taxi, (360) 376–TAXI
- Rental cars are available on San Juan Island from M & W Auto (800–323–6037, www.interisland.net/mandw).
- Susie's Mopeds (360–378–5244, www.susiesmopeds.com), located in Friday Harbor, has rental cars and mopeds for both Orcas and San Juan Islands.

away from all lodging options. Do yourself a favor and book reservations well in advance.

While the San Juans are still refreshingly free of big-name retailers, the expanding tourism industry has also brought most modern conveniences to Lopez, Orcas, and San Juan Islands. You'll find food markets with good selections in Lopez Village on Lopez Island, East Sound on Orcas Island, and Friday Harbor on San Juan Island. East Sound and Friday Harbor also have shops selling sporting goods, film, and other outdoor accessories. If you're looking for larger gear such as sleeping bags and tents, it's best to take care of business before getting out to the islands. Also be aware that prices are about 20 percent higher in the islands compared to the mainland.

Lopez Island

Odlin County Park

Just a mile from the ferry landing, Odlin County Park is a popular camping destination, with a sandy beach, dock, ballfield, picnic area, and shelter, along with mooring buoys and a launch for both hand-carried and trailer-mounted boats. The park makes a good launch spot for kayak trips along the east side of or around Shaw Island. You'll find thirty campsites here ($16 to $19 per night), including sites right on the beach, as well as more-secluded forested sites overlooking the water. Drinking water and vault toilets are also available. Reservations can be made up to ninety days in advance and are recommended for the peak summer months.

- For more information: San Juan County Parks, (360) 378–8420, www.co .san-juan.wa.us/parks. Reservations can be made by calling (360) 378–1842.

Spencer Spit State Park

Located 5 miles from the ferry landing on the east side of Lopez Island, Spencer Spit State Park has thirty-seven standard campsites ($16 per night) with flush toilets and water. Drive-in campsites are located in forest above the water. Camping is available from March through October; the park is closed to camping from November 1 to March 1. Reservations are available from May 15

Odlin County Park, Lopez Island

to September 15. The park also offers seven upland hike-in/bike-in campsites ($10) and seven beachfront walk-in sites ($16). Three Cascadia Marine Trail sites are available along the beach for those arriving by kayak or other human-powered boats. Other park facilities include a day-use shelter and kitchen area, a beachfront stone shelter, two group camps (one with an Adirondack shelter), sixteen mooring buoys, and 2 miles of hiking trails.

• For more information: Washington State Parks, (888) CAMPOUT, www.parks.wa.gov

Lopez Farm Cottages and Tent Camping

Situated on a thirty-acre farm 2.5 miles from the ferry landing, Lopez Farm Cottages offers ten forested campsites ($33 a night) along with shower facilities. Campsites come with hammocks, a barbecue, and access to a covered shelter with picnic tables and an outdoor fireplace. No children or pets are allowed. Cozy cottages for couples ($90 to $150 a night) are also available, with breakfast and hot tub.

• Lopez Farm Cottages, (800) 440–3556, www.lopezfarmcottages.com

Lopez Islander Resort and Marina

Located along Fisherman Bay, Lopez Islander Resort has camping and RV sites ($25 to $35) in an open field, with access to showers, a pool, and a Jacuzzi.

- Lopez Islander Resort: (800) 736–3434, www.lopezislander.com

Other Lodging Options

- Blue Fjord Cabins, (888) 633–0401, www.interisland.net/bluefjord
- MacKaye Harbor Inn, (888) 314–6140, www.mackayeharborinn.com
- Edenwild Inn, (800) 606–0662, www.edenwildinn.com

Orcas Island

Moran State Park

By far the largest and most popular campground on Orcas Island, scenic Moran State Park, located 15 miles from the ferry, has 151 forested campsites spread among four camping areas. The South End camps, located along the south shore of Cascade Lake, tend to be the nicest but also, not surprisingly, the most popular. Facilities include showers, flush toilets, and water. Primitive camps are also available in the park for bikers and hikers. Don't expect solitude here, as the park sees heavy use during the summer months. Reservations can be made by phone or on the Internet for sites from Memorial Day through Labor Day and are highly recommended well in advance—at other times, camping is first-come, first-served. Group camping is also available, and the Camp Moran lodge and cabins can hold up to 144 people.

- For more information: Moran State Park, (360) 376–2326 (information), (800) CAMPOUT (reservations), www.orcasisle.com/~elc/ or www.parks.wa.gov/parks/regislands.asp

Obstruction Pass Recreation Area

Far smaller and less well known than Moran State Park is Obstruction Pass Recreation Area, located a few miles west of the park. The nine campsites at Obstruction Pass can be reached by boat or by a 0.5-mile hike from the parking lot. There is no potable water at Obstruction Pass, and reservations are not accepted. All sites are first-come, first-served, and can fill in summer.

- For more information: Washington State Parks, (360) 376–2326

Doe Bay Resort

Located 21 miles from the ferry landing on the east side of Orcas Island, Doe Bay Resort completed a transformation over recent years, with ownership of

Camping at Moran State Park, Orcas Island

this private resort being passed on to new owners who are developing an ayurvedic retreat.

Aside from Moran State Park, Doe Bay offers one of the few other major camping areas on the east side of Orcas Island, with fifty campsites ($35 a night) spread around a cove, some with scenic ocean views. Rustic cabins and yurts of various sizes are also available, and reservations are recommended for camping and other lodging during summer. Visitors also have access to showers, a small communal kitchen, hot tubs, and an on-premises restaurant.

• For more information: Doe Bay Resort and Retreat, (360) 376–2291, www.doebay.com

West Beach Resort

Best known for its waterfront cabins, West Beach Resort offers sixty-two camping and RV sites in a field a short walk to the water ($25 a night), with showers, propane, groceries, water, and a Laundromat. While it's not the more secluded camping you'll find elsewhere on the island, it's a good option for budget-conscious travelers who are willing to put up with a little extra company. Advanced reservations are recommended in summer.

• For more information: West Beach Resort, (877) 937–8224, www.west beachresort.com

Other Lodging Options

- General Lodging Information for Orcas Island: (360) 376–8888, www .orcas-lodging.com
- Spring Bay Inn (360–376–5531, www.springbayinn.com) is a comfortable and rustic lodge that runs kayak trips from its Obstruction Pass location.
- Beach Haven Resort, (360) 376–2288, www.beach-haven.com
- The Inn on Orcas Island, (888) 886–1661, www.theinnonorcasisland.com
- West Beach Resort, (877) 937–8224, www.westbeachresort.com
- Inn at Ship Bay, (877) 276–7296, www.innatshipbay.com
- Lieber Haven Resort and Marina, (360) 376–2472, www.lieberhaven resort.com
- The Resort at Deer Harbor, (888) 376–4480, www.deerharbor.com
- The Homestead, Orcas Island, (360) 376–5284, www.homesteadorcas.com

San Juan Island

San Juan County Park

Located on the west side of San Juan Island north of Lime Kiln Point State Park, San Juan County Park is the only public camping area on the island. You'll find twenty campsites ($23 to $32 a night) spread across twelve water-front acres, with scenic views over Haro Strait and the chance to spot whales from spring to early fall. A few sites are set aside for bikers, kayakers, and hikers ($6.00 per person). Flush toilets and water are available, as are mooring buoys and a boat ramp. Camping is available year-round, and reservations are strongly advised. The park also makes a popular launching site for kayaks.

- For more information: San Juan County Parks, (360) 378–8420, www.co .san-juan.wa.us/parks/sanjuan.html. Reservations can be made by calling (360) 378–1842.

Lakedale Resort

Located 4.5 miles from the ferry landing on the north-central side of San Juan Island, Lakedale is the island's largest camping area, offering more than 200 campsites ($19 to $31 a night) spread around two shallow lakes. Some sites are set aside for cyclists. While some of the sites seem a little close for comfort, there's swimming and fishing in the lakes, along with boat rentals, showers, and a small store. Camping is available from March 15 to October 15. If you're arriving during the off-season or looking for more high-end lodging, the

Camping at San Juan County Park, San Juan Island

resort's new lodge offers comfortable Northwest-style rooms, or you can rent one of their cabins.

- For more information: Lakedale Resort, (800) 617–CAMP, www.lakedale.com

Snug Harbor Resort

Snug Harbor Resort is located 8.5 miles from the ferry landing on the west side of San Juan Island. Along with cabins, the resort has twelve very small upland campsites, with gas and a small store. Reservations are accepted.

- For more information: Snug Harbor Resort, (360) 378–4762, www.snug resort.com

Other Lodging Options

- San Juan Island Bed and Breakfast Association, (866) 645–3030, www .san-juan-island.net
- Friday's Historic Inn, (800) 352–2632, www.friday-harbor.com
- Friday Harbor House, (360) 378–8455, www.fridayharborhouse.com
- Friday Harbor Inn, (800) 793–4756, www.fridayharborinn.com
- Friday Harbor Suites, (800) 752–5752, www.fridayharborsuites.com
- San Juan Inn, (800) 742–8210, www.sanjuaninn.com

- Roche Harbor, (800) 451–8910, www.rocheharbor.com (includes Hotel de Haro, condos, and cottages)
- Lonesome Cove Resort, (360) 378–4477, www.lonesomecove.com
- Wharfside Bed and Breakfast, (360) 378–5661, www.fridayharborlodging.com
- Tower House Bed and Breakfast, (800) 858–4276, www.san-juan-island.com
- Hillside House Bed and Breakfast, (800) 232–4730, www.hillsidehouse.com
- Wildwood Manor, (877) 298–1144, www.wildwoodmanor.com

Shaw Island

Facilities on Shaw Island are limited, so it's a good idea to plan ahead before heading to the island. Camping at South Beach County Park offers the only lodging option, and the island's only store, the Little Portion store at the ferry landing, has limited provisions.

South Beach Park

Located about 2 miles from the ferry landing, South Beach Park has twelve campsites ($13 to $16 a night) overlooking Indian Cove, with vault toilets, water, and one of the largest sandy beaches in the San Juans. You'll also find a covered picnic shelter and wood cookstove here, and both kayaks and trailered boats can be launched from the park.

- For more information: San Juan County Parks, (360) 378–8420, www.co .san-juan.wa.us/parks/shaw.html. Reservations can be made by calling (360) 378–1842.

South Beach Park, Shaw Island

Chapter 2:
Exploring the Trails

Many visitors and admirers define the San Juan Islands by their connection to water, with hundreds of miles of shoreline and dozens of bays and inlets to discover. In fact, many boaters who visit the islands barely take time to step ashore to visit the many parks and trails. But in doing so, they're missing out on some of the best exploring the islands have to offer.

For such a small area, the San Juans have a lot to offer hikers and walkers, with an amazingly diverse range of trails of all types and degrees of difficulty. You'll find strenuous climbs to the high, open ridges of Mount Constitution, serene wandering along forested mountain streams, shoreline hikes, historic walks, and more. And while virtually all of the hikes in the San Juans are day trips, it's certainly possible to spend two or more days hiking around Moran State Park on Orcas Island alone, with an overnight stay in one of the park's designated campsites. Many hikes throughout the islands can also easily be combined with cycling or kayak trips.

While this chapter covers the many hikes on the larger and more readily accessible islands, many of the smaller islands accessible by kayak or boat, such as Stuart and Sucia Islands, also contain superb hiking opportunities. You'll find more about these islands in chapter 3, Exploring the Water.

Preparing for Your Hike

While you'll certainly not be plunging into remote wilderness when hiking in the San Juans, some basic preparedness is always a good idea. Even in summer, weather in the islands can change rapidly, from warm sun to a cold-wind-driven rain, particularly on the higher slopes of Mount Constitution. For longer hikes, it's a good idea to have rain gear handy, along with insulating, noncotton layers, as hypothermia can be a real threat any time of year.

You'll also appreciate a sturdy pair of hiking boots on some of the more strenuous trails, such as those in Moran State Park or on San Juan Island. Even the more moderate walks are often on uneven dirt paths with roots and rocks to navigate. While potable water is available at some of the trailheads and markets are available on all of the major islands, it's best to plan ahead and bring enough food and water for your trip. And if you're hiking in the late fall or winter when days are shorter, make sure to allow ample time to complete the trip during daylight hours, particularly on longer trails around Mount Constitution.

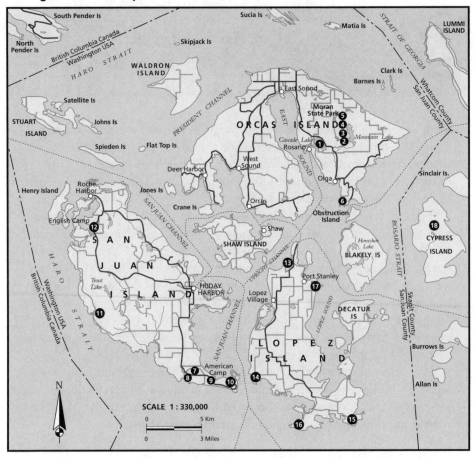

While the warm, sunny days of summer in the San Juan Islands make for great hiking, you can actually hike here year-round, thanks to the moderate climate of western Washington. Snow is rare in the islands (although more common on the summit of Mount Constitution), and you're much more likely to have a trail to yourself in late fall, winter, or early spring. Besides, there's something magical about a quiet, solitary walk through a dark, misty Pacific Northwest forest or along a rugged coastline in winter.

If you do come to Moran State Park in fall, winter, or spring, you'll find that many of the park's hiking trails are open to mountain biking as well. It's a good idea to keep an eye out for bikers if you're hiking here in the off-season.

Snapshot of the Hikes

There's something for every hiker in the San Juan Islands. Lake lovers should check out the loop trails around both **Cascade Lake** (Hike 1) and **Mountain**

Lake (Hike 3) in Moran State Park. Those looking for a thigh-burning workout rewarded by views should head to the **Mountain Lake–Mount Constitution Loop** (Hike 4) on Orcas Island, or **Jakle's Lagoon–Mount Finlayson Loop** (Hike 9) and **Mount Young** (Hike 12) on San Juan Island. Want to learn a little history? Then check out the **American Camp Interpretive Loop** (Hike 8) or **Bell Point** (Hike 12) in American and English Camps on San Juan Island. Forest lovers will appreciate the **Cold Springs–Mount Constitution Loop** (Hike 5) and **Cascade Creek Trail** (Hike 2) in Moran

State Park, as well as the short **Little Bird Trail** and **Big Tree Loop** (Hike 13) on Lopez Island. The wild, windswept south shore of Lopez Island can be experienced in walks to **Shark Reef** (Hike 14), **Watmough Bay** or **Point Colville** (Hike 15), or by a combination kayak-and-hiking trip to **Iceberg Point** (Hike 16). Whale watchers will enjoy **Lime Kiln Point** (Hike 11), while **Obstruction Pass** (Hike 6), **Spencer Spit** (Hike 17), and **South Beach** (Hike 7) provide scenic shoreline access. And if you're really looking to get away from the crowds, check out the miles of trails on wild **Cypress Island** (Hike 18).

Orcas Island

When it comes to hiking in the San Juans, Orcas Island steals the show, and for good reason: You'll find here mountainous terrain, lush forests dotted with lakes and waterfalls, and by far the most extensive and easily accessible hiking opportunities in the islands. Virtually all of the hiking is found on the 30 miles of trails in Moran State Park, where you can easily spend a few days exploring on foot and still not cover all of the trails. You'll find gentle, level strolls around one of the park's lakes as well as strenuous climbs up the steep slopes of Mount Constitution. Obstruction Pass, located south of Moran State Park, also offers a short hike out to a scenic pebble beach.

Moran State Park is a true treasure in the San Juan Islands. Opening in 1921 with a generous donation of land from Robert Moran, the park has expanded to cover more than 5,000 acres. You'll also find many signs of the 1930s-era Civilian Conservation Corps here, a government-sponsored program whose participants built many foot trails, roads, and bridges in the park, along with twenty-one buildings. Perhaps best known is the tower on top of Mount

Constitution, patterned after watchtowers in the Caucasus Mountains of southeastern Europe.

The park protects valuable habitat for wildlife. Blacktail deer, muskrats, and raccoons are abundant in and around Moran State Park, and in the winter Cascade Lake fills with waterfowl. A portion of the park contains the Mount Pickett Reserve, with the largest continuous tract of natural forest in the Puget Sound lowlands. The reserve is closed to all but organized scientific programs to protect this ecologically valuable area.

If you're coming to Moran State Park for an extended period, you'll find many other amenities here too. The park's day-use area includes picnic sites, kitchen shelters, bathhouses, boat launch areas, boat rentals, and a swimming area. Day-use areas are open year-round, and park hours are from 8:00 A.M. to dusk from October 1 to March 31, and from 6:30 A.M. to dusk from April 1 to September 30. Leashed pets are also permitted in the park. See chapter 2 for more on camping in the park.

For More Information

- Moran State Park, (360) 376–2326, www.parks.wa.gov/parks/regislands.asp

- Gnat's Nature Hikes (360–376–6629, www.orcasislandhikes.com) offers guided hikes throughout Moran State Park, where you'll learn about natural history and plant life.

The Legacy of Robert Moran

Perhaps no other person left a greater legacy of conservation in the San Juan Islands than Robert Moran. Facing failing health at the age of forty-six, the shipbuilder, businessman, and former Seattle mayor moved to Orcas Island in 1905, buying up 7,000 acres and building a grand estate, now part of Rosario Resort, for his retirement. But some say that Moran, close friends with Sierra Club founder John Muir, had conservation on his mind as much as retirement, and in 1921 he donated much of his land, which would later become Moran State Park, to the state of Washington. Moran's efforts laid the foundation for today's strong conservation ethic in the islands, including the very active and successful land preservation movement.

1 Cascade Lake Loop

WHAT TO EXPECT: A pleasant, mostly level loop that hugs the shore of Cascade Lake, with views of the slopes of Mount Constitution and of the "Lagoon" on the west shore of the lake.

GRADE: Easy due to the gentle terrain

APPROXIMATE LENGTH: 3-mile loop

APPROXIMATE TIME: 1.5 hours

GETTING THERE: From the Orcas Landing ferry dock, turn left after exiting the ferry and drive Orcas Road (Horseshoe Highway) 7 miles, bearing right at a signed junction toward Moran State Park and the village of East Sound. Continue straight ahead past Crescent Beach, then turn right onto Olga Road. At 14 miles from the ferry, you'll reach the stone arch marking the entrance to Moran State Park, and in less than 1 mile, you'll reach Cascade Lake. The trail starts from the Cascade Lake picnic area. Parking is available along both sides of the road.

The Hike

One of the most popular hikes in Moran State Park follows the wide, well-graded and scenic trail that loops its way around Cascade Lake. You'll closely

Bridge over the Lagoon at Cascade Lake, Moran State Park

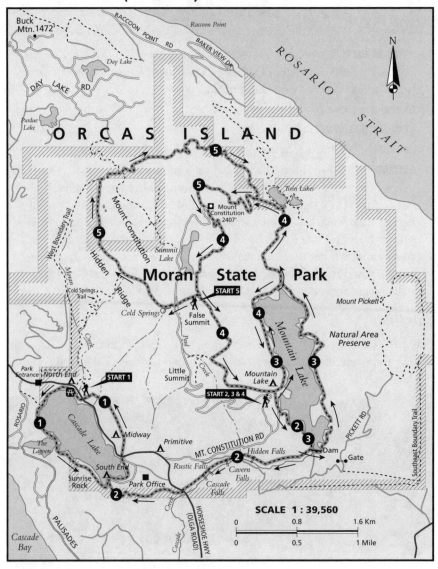

hug the shoreline for most of the way, with scenic views across the lake, especially inviting for an early morning or evening stroll. On a hot summer day, the close-at-hand lake will tempt you for a swim along the way.

Starting at the north end of the picnic area, the trail heads north then west along the lakeshore, quickly reaching a junction at 0.25 mile with a spur trail leading right to the North End Campground. It's also the first of many trails

Pacific Madrone

Throughout the San Juan Islands, you'll commonly spot the Pacific madrone. This tree, which grows from British Columbia south to Southern California and Mexico, is particularly common west of the Cascades in Washington on relatively hot, dry, and rocky sites. Typically 50 to 80 feet tall, this broad-leaved tree is most easily distinguished by its beautiful exfoliating bark, which leaves behind a smooth, polished-looking trunk with a distinctive deep reddish color on older trees. The glossy, leathery leaves, dark green above and paler green below, are arranged alternately on the stem. Native Americans used the bark and leaves as a natural astringent.

you'll encounter that connect Moran State Park to the nearby Rosario Resort. Continue straight ahead.

At just under 0.5 mile, you might notice a curiously shaped Douglas fir tree that hangs out over the lake. Its twisted, stunted appearance is not only intriguing, but you'll also find telltale signs that it's a favorite swimming spot. You'll soon pass another junction, staying left at a spur trail bearing right to Rosario Road, and left again at another junction at 0.8 mile, just before reaching a wooden bridge over the Lagoon, an inlet at the west end of the lake. The inlet was created when Cascade Lake was dammed and water levels were raised to provide hydroelectric power for Rosario. You'll find a concrete powerhouse here, still supplying 125 kilowatts of power for Rosario's outdoor lights and heat.

After passing yet another final spur trail leading right to Rosario just after the Lagoon bridge, you may notice a distinct change in vegetation on this side of the lake, where cool, mossy forests grow in contrast to the dry bluffs on the north end of the lake.

Crossing a small footbridge, you'll reach the South End Campground at 1.5 miles. For a worthwhile side diversion, turn right here for a short but thigh-burning climb for 0.3 mile to Sunrise Rock, where good views over Cascade Lake and the forested slopes of Mount Constitution await you.

To continue around the lake, walk along the road through the South End Campground for 0.1 mile and watch for a HIKERS ONLY sign bearing left from the road along a marshy cove of the lake. At 1.8 miles you'll turn right and meet Olga Road, the main road through the park. Turn left and walk along the road for about 300 feet and then cross the road, where you'll once again pick up the trail. At the next trail junction, signed for Cascade Falls, turn left, descend a short hill, and cross a stream, shortly after emerging on a gravel road. Turn right along this road, and then quickly left at a small TRAIL sign. From here, you'll descend through forest, returning to your starting point on Cascade Lake.

2 Cascade Creek

See map on page 34

WHAT TO EXPECT: A lush stream valley with old-growth forest and a series of cascading waterfalls

GRADE: Moderate due to occasional steep descents along Cascade Creek

APPROXIMATE LENGTH: 2.5 miles one-way with a car or bike shuttle, or 5 miles out and back

APPROXIMATE TIME: 1.5 hours one-way

GETTING THERE: From the Orcas Landing ferry dock, turn left after exiting the ferry and drive Orcas Road (Horseshoe Highway) 7 miles, bearing right at a signed junction toward Moran State Park and the village of East Sound. Continue straight ahead past Crescent Beach, then turn right onto Olga Road. At 14 miles from the ferry, you'll reach the stone arch marking the entrance to Moran State Park. You can access the Cascade Creek Trail from trailheads at three locations: Mountain Lake, Cascade Lake, or Cascade Falls. For the Mountain Lake trailhead, drive through the stone archway at the park entrance and past Cascade Lake, bearing left at 1.5 miles onto Mount Constitution Road. In 1 mile you'll take the right spur road to Mountain Lake. Find the signed trailhead adjacent to the parking area overlooking the lake, across from the group picnic shelter.

The Hike

Plunging through lush forest along a pretty mountain stream, you may find yourself forgetting that you're on an island surrounded by salt water. The Cascade Creek Trail is one of the few streamside hikes you'll find in the San Juan Islands, following Cascade Creek from the outlet of Mountain Lake to Cascade

Cascade Creek and Cascade Falls, Moran State Park, Orcas Island

Lake. And while much of Orcas Island's forest was harvested in the logging boom following World War II, here you'll find some of the largest remaining trees in the park. Along the way you'll pass scenic Cascade Falls, along with two other waterfalls, as the stream tumbles its way down the steep valley.

There are several ways to reach the trail along Cascade Creek—this route starts high, at Mountain Lake, and descends 570 feet to Cascade Lake. Leave a car or bike at Cascade Lake, or arrange to be picked up if you want to save yourself the climb back up to Mountain Lake.

From the trailhead, the trail winds along the rugged southwest shore of Mountain Lake, quickly passing a mountain-biking trail at 0.3 mile (stay left here) and reaching the lake's outlet dam in about 0.5 mile.

After crossing below the dam, you'll find the Cascade Creek Trail on your right. The trail descends along the stream, the cool, forested canyon and sound of the stream quickly enveloping you. Unlike many other parts of the San Juan Islands, loggers spared many of the trees here, and you'll find some enormous western red cedar and Douglas fir trees that are 300 to 400 years old. Stop and notice the large Sitka spruce trees also growing along the trail here, easily identifiable by their stiff needles that are prickly when grabbed. This majestic tree is common along Washington's outer coast, but found only in wetter sites in the relatively drier climate of the San Juan Islands.

At 1.5 miles you'll cross a footbridge and for a short time join the dirt Pickett Road, a popular route for mountain bikers. Turn right (north) along the road, and in 0.25 mile quickly turn left, following a sign for Cavern, Rustic, and Cascade Falls. You'll reach Cavern Falls in a forest of western red cedar and Douglas fir, then Rustic Falls at 1.75 miles.

The last and largest falls are Cascade Falls, gracefully tumbling 75 feet and surrounded by lush vegetation. You can view the falls from a split rail fence above—here, a spur trail to your right also leads to the Cascade Falls trailhead just off Mount Constitution Road. To continue on to the main trail's end at Cascade Lake, you'll continue downhill, where you can stop to view the falls from below. From here, cross Cascade Creek on a footbridge, soon after reaching Olga Road across from the South End Campground and the end of your trip. If you haven't arranged for a shuttle, simply retrace your steps back to the Mountain Lake trailhead.

Mountain Lake Loop

See map on page 34

WHAT TO EXPECT: A pleasant loop around the forested shores of Mountain Lake, with abundant views across the lake and to the rugged east face of Mount Constitution

GRADE: Easy due to minimal elevation gain

APPROXIMATE LENGTH: 3.5-mile loop

APPROXIMATE TIME: 1.5 hours

GETTING THERE: From the Orcas Landing ferry dock, turn left after exiting the ferry and drive Orcas Road (Horseshoe Highway) 7 miles, bearing right at a signed junction toward Moran State Park and the village of East Sound. Continue straight ahead past Crescent Beach, then turn right onto Olga Road. At 14 miles from the ferry, you'll reach the stone arch marking the entrance to Moran State Park. Drive through the stone archway at the park entrance and past Cascade Lake, bearing left at 1.5 miles onto Mount Constitution Road. In 1 mile you'll take the right spur road to Mountain Lake. Find the signed trailhead adjacent to the parking area overlooking the lake, across from the group picnic shelter.

Mountain Lake, Moran State Park, Orcas Island

Other Trails of Moran State Park

While not included in this book's hike descriptions, you may also be tempted to explore some of the other trails in Moran State Park. Here's what to expect:

- **Southeast Boundary Trail:** This mostly forested trail accesses the park's southeast corner. More popular with mountain bikers in summer, the rough trail is not regularly maintained, offering only limited views to the east toward Mount Baker. Total trail length is about 3 miles one-way, bisected by a spur trail from Pickett Road at about 1.75 miles.

- **Cold Springs Trail:** This trail climbs steeply along Cold Creek for 2.7 miles from Cascade Lake's North End Campground, gaining 1,700 feet along the way. Crossing Cold Creek a few times, views from the trail are largely limited.

- **West Boundary Trail:** Known locally as the Powerline Trail, this seldom-used trail follows—you guessed it—powerlines to the junction with the North Trail. Steep and unforgiving, it offers a grueling workout, but you'll find better scenery on other park trails.

The Hike

Mountain Lake, the larger and wilder of Moran State Park's two lakes, makes for a serene setting, its deep blue waters inviting for a swim on a warm summer day. Like Cascade Lake, Mountain Lake wasn't always so large, the lake's dam raising its level to supply water to the communities of Olga and Doe Bay on the east end of the island.

This mainly level trail makes a pleasant loop around Mountain Lake under the cool shade of forest, with frequent views of the lake and rugged eastern slopes of Mount Constitution. While you can walk either way around the lake, this hike starts by heading south to the south end of the lake and then north along its east shore.

Start your hike at the trailhead just south of the Mountain Lake Campground and group shelter, at the south end of the small parking area overlooking the lake. You'll follow the trail along and above the rugged lakeshore, staying left at your first trail junction with a mountain-biking trail to the right.

In 0.5 mile you'll reach the lake's dam and cross below the dam on the trail. In the late 1890s, about nine families lived around the lake before Robert Moran bought them out as part of his effort to establish a state park. Moran then had the lake's original dam built in 1905 to provide a more reliable water supply for his Rosario home. It was then raised 3.5 feet in 1948 to provide water for Doe Bay and Olga.

Here, you'll pass the trail for Cascade Creek on your right. Continue straight ahead, heading around the lake, ignoring yet another spur trail that connects with the Mount Pickett Trail.

Along the east side of the lake, you'll get good views of Mount Constitution, including the main summit and rugged cliffs on the east side of the mountain. Cliffs such as these are not only scenic, they also provide habitat for a variety of raptors.

Just over 2 miles from the trailhead, you'll reach the north end of Mountain Lake and a junction with the Twin Lakes Trail leading to the right (north). This trail leads to Twin Lakes and then on to the summit of Mount Constitution. Instead, you'll continue around Mountain Lake.

Heading south along the west shore of Mountain Lake, the trail is pleasant and level, with constant views over the lake. At 2.8 miles, keep an eye out for a large rock along the lakeshore, an inviting spot for a rest, or perhaps even a quick swim (also check out the rope swing here). You'll reach the end of the trail at the Mountain Lake Campground and Bonnie Sliger Memorial trailhead after 3.5 miles. Simply follow the road a short distance back to the parking lot and your starting trailhead.

4 Mountain Lake– Mount Constitution Loop

See map on page 34

WHAT TO EXPECT: A strenuous, 7-mile loop that climbs past lakes to the glorious summit of Mount Constitution, along its airy ridgetop, and back to Mountain Lake

GRADE: Strenuous due to steep terrain and elevation gain

APPROXIMATE LENGTH: 7-mile loop

APPROXIMATE TIME: 4 hours

GETTING THERE: From the Orcas Landing ferry dock, turn left after exiting the ferry and drive Orcas Road (Horseshoe Highway) 7 miles, bearing right at a signed junction toward Moran State Park and the village of East Sound. Continue straight ahead past Crescent Beach, then turn right onto Olga Road. At 14 miles from the ferry, you'll reach the stone arch marking the entrance to Moran State Park. Drive through the stone archway at the park entrance and past Cascade Lake, bearing left at 1.5 miles onto Mount Constitution Road. In 1 mile you'll take the right spur road to

Mountain Lake. Find the signed trailhead adjacent to the parking area overlooking the lake, across from the group picnic shelter.

The Hike

In contrast to the easy strolls you'll find in other parts of Moran State Park, this hike will give you a good workout, along with a sampling of the park's lakes, streams, and glorious views from the summit of Mount Constitution. While large sections of the route are level, you'll also have to contend with a steep climb of nearly 1,500 feet to the summit, making this one of the more strenuous trails in the park. Sure, you can drive to the top, but sometimes views earned by getting there on foot are just that much more satisfying.

This route pieces together portions of several trails to create a loop trip of approximately 7 miles. You can travel the hike in either direction, or even start the loop at other intermediate points along the route, including Little Summit, Cold Springs, or the Mount Constitution summit itself, although if you do, you'll miss out on a swim in Mountain Lake at the end. It's most enjoyable to climb the summit via the Twin Lakes Trail, and to descend back to Mountain Lake on the sometimes-rough trail from Little Summit to Mountain Lake.

The trail starts at the Bonnie Sliger Memorial trailhead, found by walking from the parking area overlooking Mountain Lake past the day-use shelter to its end at the Mountain Lake Campground. You'll start out along the forested shores of Mountain Lake, the first mile a pleasant, level stroll with views of the lake through the forest. Several side trails will tempt you to the lakeshore for a scenic rest stop. At 1.3 miles you'll cross a footbridge, reaching a junction—the trail to the right continues around the lake to complete the Mountain Lake Loop.

Instead, you'll turn left here and gently climb a scenic forested valley toward Twin Lakes along a pretty spring-fed stream, one of several flowing into Mountain Lake. At just over 2 miles, you'll reach a junction at the marshy shores of Upper Twin Lake. To add about a mile to your total trip, turn right here, where short spur trails lead around Upper Twin (0.6 mile) and Lower Twin (0.4 mile) Lakes, both fed from among the many springs on Orcas Island.

To continue toward the summit from the junction, bear left, quickly starting the steady 1.5-mile climb up the east slopes of Mount Constitution. Continue straight ahead past a junction with the North Trail, which leads to the right to Cold Springs. The trail soon steepens and starts the relentless climb, switching back several times as it steadily grinds higher up the forested slopes. Views through the trees tempt you with what's to come at the summit.

Finally, after 1.5 long miles from Twin Lakes, you'll reach the summit parking area, where you'll turn left, walk through the parking area, and find the short trail leading to the summit lookout.

Summit of Mount Constitution, Moran State Park, Orcas Island

Leave plenty of time to take in the sweeping, magnificent views both near and far from the summit rocks. For even better views, climb the historic look-out tower, constructed during the Civilian Conservation Corps era in 1939. Look to the east, past the forested slopes and farms of Lummi Island to the snowy mass of Mount Baker floating on the horizon. Watch the tiny boats below you ply past Clark and Barnes Islands and, on clear days, pick out the tiny skyline of Vancouver to the north or the slopes of Mount Rainier, more than 120 miles to the south. Gaze north across the Strait of Georgia, past Sucia and Matia Islands to Vancouver Island.

When you've finally soaked in your fill of the views, you'll retrace your steps to the summit parking lot and turn left, picking up the Little Summit Trail behind the restroom building. Along with the views to the east and south as you descend along the dry, open summit ridge, the trail also offers a good lesson in forest ecology. Note here the difference between these trees and the lush forest found elsewhere in the park. Here, the forest is dominated by lodgepole pine, a tree more frequently found in drier intermountain areas east of Washington's Cascade Mountains. In fact, you're walking through one of the largest lodge-pole pine forests in western Washington, supported by just the right combination of soils, temperature, and rainfall. Also keep an eye out for lilies, asters, and stonecrop growing on the grassier south slopes of the mountain.

At just over 1 mile from the summit, you'll reach an intersection, with the right spur leading quickly to Mount Constitution Road and the Cold Springs parking area (another option for starting your loop here). Instead, you'll turn left and continue descending the summit ridge, where you'll reach an intersection again in another 0.9 mile. The trail descending to the left leads toward your starting trailhead at Mountain Lake.

For a short side trip, continue straight ahead a short 0.3 mile to Little Summit, which offers enticing views of the Olympics and Mount Rainier to the south, then retrace your steps to the intersection. From the intersection it's another 0.8 mile of steep descent, dropping nearly 1,300 feet to your starting point at Mountain Lake.

5 Cold Springs–Mount Constitution Loop

See map on page 34

WHAT TO EXPECT: A traverse through grand forests high on the north slopes of Mount Constitution, crossing over the summit and down along its scenic ridgetop

GRADE: Strenuous due to steep terrain and elevation gain

APPROXIMATE LENGTH: 5-mile loop

APPROXIMATE TIME: 3 hours

GETTING THERE: From the Orcas Landing ferry dock, turn left after exiting the ferry and drive Orcas Road (Horseshoe Highway) 7 miles, bearing right at a signed junction toward Moran State Park and the village of East Sound. Continue straight ahead past Crescent Beach, then turn right onto Olga Road. At 14 miles from the ferry, you'll reach the stone arch marking the entrance to Moran State Park. Drive through the stone archway at the park entrance and past Cascade Lake, bearing left at 1.5 miles onto Mount Constitution Road. Continue past the turnoff for Mountain Lake, reaching in 3.5 miles the parking area for Cold Springs and a gate on the left side of the road.

The Hike

This "high route" circumnavigates the upper slopes of Mount Constitution, climbing the summit ridge. And while it doesn't offer the same up-close lake views as the loop from Mountain Lake, you'll find fewer ups and downs on this trail, starting high at the Cold Springs trailhead and passing through forest much of the way. It's generally less frequently used, leaving you to wander quietly past the cathedral-like trees on the north slopes of Mount Constitution.

Cold Springs shelter, Moran State Park, Orcas Island

Starting at the Cold Springs trailhead, the trail quickly passes the Cold Springs shelter, an impressive example of Civilian Conservation Corps–era architecture from the 1930s, when government-sponsored camps came to build many of today's roads, trails, and historic structures in the park. Just past the shelter you'll find Cold Springs itself, which supplied water for a campground that existed here until the early 1970s.

After passing a few wetlands along the trail, in less than a mile you'll reach an intersection with the Cold Springs Trail to the left, descending 2.5 miles steeply back to Cascade Lake by a series of switchbacks. Instead, you'll bear right on the North Trail under a dense canopy of lodgepole pine, around the west side of Mount Constitution.

At 1.5 miles from the trailhead, you'll cross the West Boundary Trail, which follows the swath of rather unsightly powerlines up the slopes of Mount Constitution from the north end of Cascade Lake. Ducking back into the forest, the trail traverses the west and north slopes of Mount Constitution. Note some of the stonework supporting the trail on the mountain's steep slopes here, more evidence of the impressive work performed by the Civilian Conservation Corps.

After a pleasant walk through grand forests of Douglas fir, western red cedar, and hemlock, at 2.4 miles you'll reach the intersection with the Twin Lakes Trail, which descends to the left a quick 0.3 mile to Twin Lakes.

You'll continue 1.5 miles toward Mount Constitution, the trail soon steepening and switching back several times as it steadily grinds higher up the forested slopes. Reaching the summit parking area, turn left, walk through the parking area, and find the short trail leading to the summit lookout.

From the summit retrace your steps to the summit parking lot and turn left, picking up the Little Summit Trail behind the restroom building. At the intersection with the Cold Springs Trail in just over a mile, simply turn right, quickly reaching the road and your starting point.

6 Obstruction Pass

WHAT TO EXPECT: A short 0.5-mile walk through forest to a pebbly beach with views over Obstruction Pass

GRADE: Easy due to short length and minimal elevation change

APPROXIMATE LENGTH: 1 mile out and back

APPROXIMATE TIME: 1 hour

GETTING THERE: From the Orcas Landing ferry dock, turn left after exiting the ferry and drive Orcas Road (Horseshoe Highway) 7 miles,

Beach at Obstruction Pass, Orcas Island

Obstruction Pass

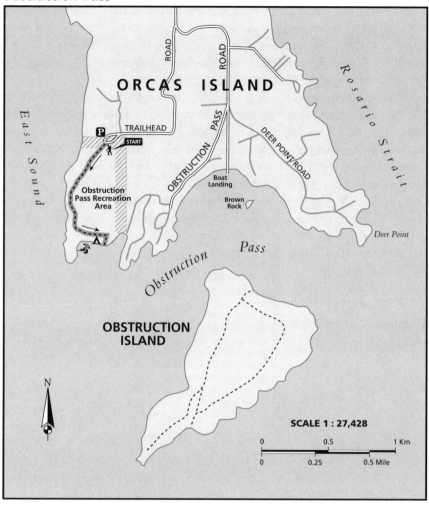

bearing right at a signed junction toward Moran State Park and the village of East Sound. Continue straight ahead past Crescent Beach, then turn right onto Olga Road. At 14 miles from the ferry, you'll reach the stone arch marking the entrance to Moran State Park. Drive through the park on Olga Road to the intersection with Point Lawrence Road. Turn left onto Point Lawrence Road, and in 0.75 mile turn right (south) onto Obstruction Pass Road. In 0.8 mile turn right onto the gravel Trailhead Road and follow it to its end at the trailhead.

The Hike

This short trail leads 0.5 mile from the Obstruction Pass parking area to a lovely pebble beach and the Obstruction Pass Recreation Area. The trail makes for a pleasant morning or afternoon walk, with the added option of camping overnight at the small campground above the beach. Along the way, the nearly level trail wanders through forest, then along high bluffs with views over East Sound. You'll pass an occasional spur trail that leads out to outlooks along the way before reaching the campground in 0.5 mile.

While there are ample hiking opportunities on Orcas Island, the lack of shoreline access has always been the subject of frustration for water lovers here. Obstruction Pass is among the more secluded public beaches on Orcas Island reachable by land, where you can explore the tide pools, or just pull up a piece of driftwood and watch the changing currents offshore. It's also a good stop for kayakers on longer trips through the islands, or for even a day trip.

If you're willing to pack your gear the short distance from the parking area, Obstruction Pass also makes a good camping alternative to the larger Moran State Park, which can certainly be less than tranquil on busy summer weekends. The nine campsites, however, are first-come, first-served, and often fill up during summer months.

For More Information

Washington State Parks, (360) 376–2326, www.parks.wa.gov/parks/regis lands.asp

San Juan Island

While Moran State Park on Orcas Island grabs the spotlight when it comes to hiking in the San Juans, San Juan Island's hiking opportunities definitely shouldn't be overlooked. While not as extensive as Orcas Island, you'll arguably find a more diverse array of hiking on San Juan Island's trails, from seashore walks and historic interpretive trails to saltwater lagoons and breezy hilltops. Most hiking is concentrated on the west side of the island, in and around the two units of the San Juan Island National Historical Park, and around Lime Kiln Point State Park.

San Juan Island National Historical Park consists of two units, American Camp on the southwest side of the island and English Camp (also sometimes called British Camp) on the northwest side. It's easy to spend a full day exploring American Camp, while English Camp can be enjoyed in an afternoon. No overnight camping is provided, and pets must be leashed. Both units are open daily from dawn until 11:00 P.M.

It's worth a stop at the park's main visitor center at American Camp, which describes in more detail the origins of the Pig War boundary dispute, camp life, and the archaeology of the park. The center is open daily from 8:30 A.M. to 5:00 P.M. during the summer, and Thursday through Sunday 8:30 A.M. to 4:30 P.M. from September through June.

For More Information

San Juan Island National Historical Park, (360) 378–2240, www.nps.gov/sajh

Creating a Walkable San Juan Island

Even with all of the hiking opportunities on San Juan Island, some local islanders have an even greater goal in mind: a more "walkable" island, not just for hikers, but for all of its residents. Their vision includes a network of paths connecting towns, destinations, and major attractions across the island, for locals and visitors alike. Since 1999 the San Juan Island Trails Committee, formed by local volunteers, has been documenting all of the island's trails and cooperating with managers of all the trails on public lands as well as around Roche Harbor. A handy reference for all of the island's walking opportunities can be found at www.sanjuanislandtrails.org.

WHAT TO EXPECT: Wander along open bluffs overlooking Haro Strait to the longest beach in the San Juan Islands

GRADE: Easy due to minimal elevation change

APPROXIMATE LENGTH: 3 miles out and back

APPROXIMATE TIME: 1.5 hours

GETTING THERE: From the ferry terminal in Friday Harbor, drive south out of town on Mullis Street until it becomes Cattle Point Road. Drive south on Cattle Point Road 4 miles from Friday Harbor, past False Bay Drive. Cattle Point Road will curve to the left, where you'll enter the American Camp unit of San Juan Island National Historical Park. Bear right and follow signs to the visitor center and trailhead.

The Hike

American Camp's 1,200 acres of shoreline, prairie grassland, and forest form a wonderful mosaic of landscapes on the south end of San Juan Island, and it's historically one of the most interesting places as well. In particular, the 1.5-mile

South Beach, American Camp, San Juan Island

American Camp and Cattle Point (Hikes 7–10)

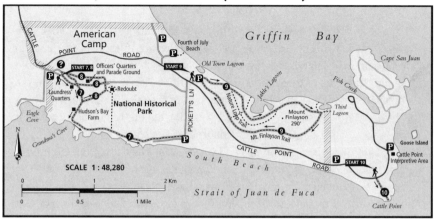

hike along the open bluffs to South Beach, the longest beach in the San Juans, makes a scenic one-way trip (with a car at the other end) or loop trip with a few options on how you return. At low tides, it's possible to walk the trails along the bluffs, then return by walking along the beach.

Whatever route you choose, you'll have sweeping views out over Haro Strait to the west, where you can keep an eye out for orca whales, Dall's porpoises, and harbor seals, or just sit and watch the boats cruising up and down the strait. On blustery fall and winter days, the open bluffs also make a good place to watch rain-swollen storm clouds sweep across the Strait of Juan de Fuca.

From the visitor center parking lot, you'll find two trails heading east, one at the north end and one at the south end of the parking lot. Both essentially head in the same direction, shortly emerging into meadow near the parade ground. To the south of the grounds, you'll find the Laundress' Quarters and a trail heading to the right (south), descending on a visible path through the meadow toward the beach.

In about 0.25 mile the trail branches both right and left along the bluffs. You'll eventually turn left (east) to head toward South Beach, but a short side trip to the right leads down to Grandma's Cove, a scenic pocket beach cupped by high bluffs worthy of some extra exploration time.

Back on the bluffs heading toward South Beach, follow any one of the primitive trails here toward your destination. Use caution along this route as rabbits have excavated holes, or "warrens," throughout the prairie. Introduced in the 1890s by settlers, the European rabbit was established as a wild animal on the island by 1895. In the 1920s and 1930s, the rabbit population soared, dropping in the 1980s, only to rise again in the 1990s. While the park has no plans to

The Pig War

It's nearly impossible to visit San Juan Island without hearing tales about the Pig War. The war was actually a several-year stalemate instigated over possession of San Juan Island, the last straw being the shooting of—you guessed it—a pig. The roots of the conflict lie in the British-American struggle over the Oregon Territory. While the Oregon Treaty of 1846 settled most matters about the territory's ownership, it was less than clear about the boundary when it came to San Juan Island, with both countries claiming the island as theirs. In June 1859 an American settler named Lyman Cutlar killed a pig out to ruin his garden that belonged to Hudson's Bay Company. The infuriated Hudson's Bay Company threatened to arrest Cutlar over the incident, causing the island's American settlers to demand protection from the British. Soon, the British sent ships and the Americans sent ships and infantry to the island, creating a joint occupation that lasted more than a decade. Finally, in 1872 German arbiter Kaiser Wilhelm I, brought in to resolve the crisis, awarded the island to the United States, ending the conflict without (pig aside) a single shot being fired. Today you'll find the history of this conflict interpreted in American and English Camps, part of the San Juan Island National Historical Park.

exterminate the furry creatures at this point, they do present somewhat of a management conundrum.

Along the bluffs you'll also pass a curious crumbling stone cairn alongside the trail. While it's unclear as to why it's here, one story is that it's a memorial to a family that died when a fisherman's shack burned down near the turn of the twentieth century.

With so many lush forests on other parts of the San Juans, you may wonder why prairies dominate so much here. Many areas have remained prairie due to a combination of exposure to direct summer sun, drying effects of the wind, and the low precipitation created by the rain shadow of the Olympic Mountains. You may even notice some fire scars as you walk, as National Park Service fire crews are completing prescribed burns in hopes of one day restoring the prairie to its natural state.

About 0.5 mile beyond the last junction, you'll find another trail heading left away from the water. If you want to cut your trip a little shorter, this trails heads north through the meadow toward the redoubt site, where you can pick up American Camp's interpretive trail and loop back to the visitor center.

Otherwise, continue along the bluffs to South Beach, about 1.5 miles total, where the trails end at the parking area. The stretch of South Beach east of

Pickett's Lane is backed by high bluffs, actually glacial moraines composed of deposits of glacial till, up to 100 feet high. You'll find a large number of shorebirds here, including terns, gulls, plovers, turnstones, and yellowlegs, along with some less common birds such as brown pelicans, sanderlings, shearwaters, and storm petrels.

From here, wander as you wish along the beach, and when you're ready you can simply retrace your steps along the bluffs, walk back at low tide along the beach, or return via the redoubt site as described earlier.

8 American Camp Interpretive Loop

See map on page 51

WHAT TO EXPECT: An easy interpretive loop sharing the rich history of American Camp and the Pig War

GRADE: Easy due to short distance and minimal elevation change

APPROXIMATE LENGTH: 1.25-mile loop

APPROXIMATE TIME: One hour

GETTING THERE: From the ferry terminal in Friday Harbor, drive south out of town on Mullis Street until it becomes Cattle Point Road. Drive south on Cattle Point Road 4 miles from Friday Harbor, past False Bay Drive. Cattle Point Road will curve to the left, where you'll enter the American Camp unit of San Juan Island National Historical Park. Bear right and follow signs to the visitor center and trailhead.

The Hike

Starting off at the visitor center gives you the opportunity to enjoy American Camp's 1.25-mile interpretive loop, winding its way through meadows just east of the center. Guided tours are offered Friday and Saturday through the summer, or simply pick up an interpretive brochure at the trailhead for your own self-guided tour.

The trail winds its way past the old parade ground, the Laundress' Quarters, and the site of the Bellevue Sheep Farm, which traded wool and other agricultural products with the Russian American Company in southeast Alaska, as well as markets in California, Mexico, and China. Walk past the Officers' Quarters, redoubts (fortifications), and earthen gun platforms. As the San Juans were little more than isolated outposts in the 1800s, it's easy to imagine the boredom, bad food, and bad winter storms the soldiers must have endured—and for twelve years!

Laundress' Quarters, American Camp, San Juan Island

Standing on the redoubt at American Camp, you can gaze south across the prairie to South Beach, over the waters of the Strait of Juan de Fuca to the Olympic Mountains, and (on a clear day) southeast to Mount Rainier. To the east is the 290-foot ridge of Mount Finlayson with the distinct line between prairie and forest visible on its slopes. To the north across Griffin Bay you can see Turtleback Mountain and Mount Constitution on Orcas Island, Shaw Island, and Lopez Island.

9 Jakle's Lagoon–Mount Finlayson Loop

See map on page 51

WHAT TO EXPECT: A moderate loop through lush forest, past several eco-logically rich lagoons to ridgetop prairie and sweeping views of the Olympics to the south and the Cascades and Mount Baker to the east

GRADE: Moderate due to modest elevation gain

APPROXIMATE LENGTH: 3-mile loop

APPROXIMATE TIME: 2 hours

GETTING THERE: From the ferry terminal in Friday Harbor, drive south out of town on Mullis Street until it becomes Cattle Point Road. Drive south on Cattle Point Road 4 miles from Friday Harbor, past False Bay Drive. Cattle Point Road will curve to the left, where you'll enter the American Camp unit of San Juan Island National Historical Park. Drive approximately 1 mile beyond the visitor center, passing Pickett's Lane on your right, and find the small trailhead parking area on your left.

The Hike

If you've got an interest in ecology, this is the hike for you. This loop hike will give you an idea of how just slight differences in landscape can result in big changes in the kind of vegetation that grows there. Here, you'll start out in lush forest and wander past quiet lagoons, then climb to a ridge to big views over windswept prairie.

The trail starts out on an abandoned fire road that's been closed to protect the area, descending through a forest of Douglas fir, hemlock, bigleaf maple, and alder. Before you start on your hike, take a moment to enjoy the view of Old Town (First) Lagoon from the trailhead, the location of the first town site on San Juan Island. Footings from the first buildings, which burned in 1890, can still be found in the grass around the lagoon. Beyond First Lagoon is Fourth of July Beach, also a pleasant and worthwhile stop accessible off Cattle Point Road.

As you start your hike, the posts you'll see along this first section of trail mark stations for the shorter interpretive loop you can do from this trailhead as well. Ask at the American Camp visitor center whether brochures are available for this shorter self-guided hike, or go to the park's Web site to download your own copy (www.nps.gov/sajh/jakle%27s_self-guided.pdf).

The moister environment of the wet coniferous forest on the north side of Mount Finlayson survives by being sheltered from the drying effects of wind and direct sun. Such closed canopy forests are most dramatic on protected north-facing slopes and interior flatlands. Douglas fir, western hemlock, salal, and sword fern are common here, while western red cedar and grand fir are also important species inhabiting such north-facing slopes.

The numerous side trails you'll encounter along this trail can be a little confusing—many of the spur trails to the left simply dead-end at the water's edge on Griffin Bay. At one of the first intersections you'll come to after about 0.3 mile, the Jakle's Farm Nature Loop trail heads off to the right; those who've come to do this short interpretive loop will turn right here.

Otherwise, continue straight ahead, heading east and downhill toward Jakle's Lagoon. You'll pass two more spur trails to the left that simply lead down to the shoreline.

Trail to Jakle's Lagoon, San Juan Island

At 0.6 mile you'll reach a four-way intersection. Turn left here onto a short spur trail to reach the lagoon, visible through the trees. You can explore among driftwood and along the beach here, enjoying the view across the sheltered waters of Griffin Bay to Lopez Island and other islands. Along with Old Town and Third Lagoons, Jakle's Lagoon is an estuarine wetland, and the three are the only temperate marine lagoons on the island, which themselves are rare along the entire Pacific Northwest coast.

To reach Third Lagoon, retrace your steps to the previous intersection and turn left (east) back onto the main trail, paralleling the shoreline toward Third Lagoon. Ignore trails you pass leading to the right. Third Lagoon is accessible by a faint trail leading to the left just under 1 mile from the main trailhead. From here the main trail continues straight ahead 0.3 mile to the boundary of the national historical park. Short trails beyond here crisscross adjacent property jointly owned by the San Juan County Land Bank and the state's Department of Natural Resources, eventually leading to Fish Creek and Cattle Point Road.

Instead, at this intersection at Third Lagoon, you'll turn right and begin the short but steep 0.3-mile climb to the ridge of Mount Finlayson, passing some impressive examples of mature western red cedar trees along this moist north slope.

When you reach the ridge crest, you'll notice the dramatic change in vegetation. While the north-facing slope is densely forested, the south-facing slope is an open prairie. Along the transition between the two, notice the twisted Douglas firs, shaped by the wind that rakes the ridgetop. The views from here are spectacular, stretching all the way from Mount Baker, Cattle Pass, and Lopez Island to the east, across Haro Strait to Vancouver Island to the west, and down to South Beach below you. The Olympic Mountains and Admiralty Inlet unfold in the distance farther to the south, and on some days you can even catch views of more distant Mount Rainier.

For more wandering, head left through the meadows, following the trail along the ridge and, if you'd like, eventually down to Cattle Point Road below you. To return to the trailhead, you'll turn right (west) here and follow the trail along the ridgetop, eventually leading back to the trailhead.

10 Cattle Point

See map on page 51

WHAT TO EXPECT: A short walk out to the scenic south tip of San Juan Island at Cattle Point

GRADE: Easy due to the short distance and minimal elevation change

APPROXIMATE LENGTH: Less than 0.5 mile out and back

APPROXIMATE TIME: 30 minutes

GETTING THERE: From the ferry terminal in Friday Harbor, drive south out of town on Mullis Street until it becomes Cattle Point Road. Drive

Cattle Point, San Juan Island

south on Cattle Point Road 4 miles from Friday Harbor, past False Bay Drive. Cattle Point Road will curve to the left, where you'll enter the American Camp unit of San Juan Island National Historical Park. Drive past the visitor center on Cattle Point Road approximately 2.5 miles, finding the trailhead where the road turns to the left. Parking is available along the road 0.25 mile before reaching the trailhead, or just beyond at the Cattle Point Interpretive Area. To reach the trail to Cattle Point, simply walk back a short distance along the road.

The Hike

Encompassing Cattle Point itself is the Cattle Point Natural Resources Conservation Area, where you'll find a short 0.2-mile trail out to the Cattle Point Lighthouse, built in 1935. The area is managed by the state's Department of Natural Resources to protect its sensitive resources and to provide low-impact public use. As one of the driest places in the San Juans, the area provides a unique mix of habitats that draws several species of butterflies to the host plants here. Goldfinches also nest here later in the summer season when thistle and Queen Anne's lace go to seed, and it's not uncommon to spot eagles. Stay on the marked trails to protect this fragile conservation area.

Just north of Cattle Point along Cattle Point Road is the Cattle Point Interpretive Area. Here you'll find more views over Cattle Pass, along with the remnants of a building that served as a radio compass station for Navy ships navigating the Strait of Juan de Fuca during World War II. Excavations by archaeologists in this area, one of the most extensively studied Native American sites on the island, show that it was also an important fishing site for Native Americans. Extensive shell middens (thick concentrations of artifacts) found here suggest that it was used by Native Americans for summer fishing and shellfish gathering and was occupied as long as 9,000 years ago.

Along the shore the turbulent current in Cattle Pass attracts numerous birds including Pacific loons, grebes, cormorants, and sea ducks. Tiny Goose Island, just offshore, is owned by The Nature Conservancy and provides habitat for breeding harbor seals. It's a great place to just sit and watch the waves crashing against the rocks, or the boats navigating the strong currents of Cattle Pass.

For More Information

Washington Department of Natural Resources, Northwest Region, Sedro-Woolley, Washington, (360) 856–3500

11 Lime Kiln Point State Park

WHAT TO EXPECT: A short loop along the west shore of San Juan Island, where you can spot whales and learn about the past at the historic lighthouse and lime kiln operation

GRADE: Easy due to the short distance and minimal elevation change

APPROXIMATE LENGTH: 1-mile loop

APPROXIMATE TIME: 1 hour

GETTING THERE: From the ferry landing, drive Spring Street through the town of Friday Harbor, which will turn into San Juan Valley Road. Turn left onto Douglas Road and then right onto Bailer Hill Road. This becomes West Side Road, which will lead you to Lime Kiln Point State Park, about 9 miles from the ferry landing.

The Hike

Better known as a whale-watching destination than a hiking area, Lime Kiln Point State Park offers a short loop hike that's full of both cultural and natural history. During the summer Lime Kiln Point is often jammed with visitors who come to watch the orca whales feeding offshore. Whether or not the whales

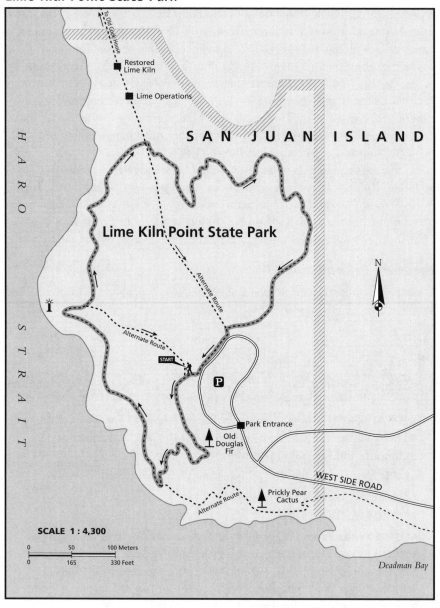

make an appearance, take the time to do this pleasant 1-mile loop. You'll find a self-guiding interpretive brochure at the trailhead. It's also possible to do a larger (but poorly marked) 2-mile loop from Lime Kiln Point State Park past the lime kilns, through the old lime quarry, past Deadman Bay, and back to the park.

From the parking lot, the interpretive trail heads west and south, passing several interpretive stations and signs. Along the way you'll learn about the

The Fate of the Orcas

The waters around the San Juans are home to the orca whale, *Orcinus orca*. Orcas have captured the human imagination through popular films and aquariums, and whale watching has become a major tourist draw for the San Juans. Many visitors come each summer with just one objective: to witness these majestic creatures in their natural environment.

The eighty-five or so orcas off San Juan Island, part of the region's "Southern Resident" population, are part of three distinct family groups, or "pods"— the J, K, and L pods. So studied are these animals that researchers have come to know each individual, giving them names such as "Granny," "Ruffles," and "Mega." Each whale is also recognizable by its distinct dorsal fin. While the J pod inhabits the area year-round, you're most likely to spot the three pods of whales between May and September, when the orcas arrive to feed on salmon, which make up over 90 percent of their diet, that migrate through the rich waters of Haro Strait. And while they'll be busy feeding most of the time, the orcas can at times put on quite a show. You may spot an orca swimming in to shore for a closer look at you, or perhaps playfully breaching just offshore. You can even listen to their calls on a local radio station, linked to an underwater microphone off Lime Kiln Point.

There's been much concern recently about the fate of the Southern Resident orcas, and increasing worry about recent population declines. Historically reviled by fishermen as competitors for the region's salmon catch or seen as a commodity to be captured and taken to aquariums, support for the whales has grown since the early 1970s. In May 2003 the population was listed as "depleted" under the federal Marine Mammal Protection Act, and further protections are still being debated. Nobody knows for sure what's causing their decline. Some blame chemicals such as PCBs, banned but still prevalent in the marine environment. Others point to declining salmon runs, or even underwater military testing. Still others blame the expanding whale-watching industry, which opponents claim interrupts the whale's feeding and resting behavior. Already among the most studied marine mammal populations in the world, researchers continue to search for answers to the orcas' future.

area's forests, many of which were cut to fuel the adjacent lime kiln, although a few larger individual trees remain. Snowberry, oceanspray, and hairy honeysuckle dominate the forest understory here.

As you reach the picnic area near the shoreline, keep an eye out for the prickly pear cactus, which may seem like a strange contrast to the cool, damp forests found on much of the San Juans. This species, distinguished by its

Old lime kiln at Lime Kiln Point State Park, San Juan Island

paddlelike leaves and yellow flowers in midsummer, grows on south-facing outcrops where soils are thin and dry, although its numbers have been declining in
the San Juan Islands. A spur trail heading left (south) from the picnic area along
the shore toward Deadman Bay offers the best chance to spot one of them, and
to explore the tide pools in search of purple sea stars, limpets, colorful
anemones, and hermit crabs.

From the picnic area, the trail turns north and follows the rugged shoreline
to the Lime Kiln Point Lighthouse. Take the time for a guided tour of this historic landmark, listed on the National Register of Historic Places, and to learn

more about the orca whales. (The view from the top isn't so bad either.) Tours are offered mainly on Saturday in the summer months.

A short spur trail from the lighthouse heads directly back to the parking lot, while the main interpretive trail continues north along the shoreline. The next major stop along the trail is the site of the historic lime kiln operations, reached from a short spur trail leading left (north) off the main trail. The San Juan Lime Company began their operations here in 1860, and at one time shipped lime, an important element in cement, from a dock here as far as San Francisco to help rebuild the ravaged city following the 1906 earthquake. Thanks to the San Juan County Land Bank, an adjacent piece of property containing another lime kiln and the "Old Cook House" has also been protected and is accessible by following a small trail past the lime kilns.

Once you've retraced your steps to the main trail, you can complete the interpretive trail, which loops into the forest and back to the parking lot, or simply take the more direct trail back to the parking lot. Along the interpretive trail route, at about 0.2 mile from the Lime Kiln intersection, you'll find a spur trail leading to the left. This connects with several short loop and spur trails that wind through the Land Bank property and to the West Side Road above you.

For More Information

The Whale Museum, Friday Harbor, Washington, (360) 378–4710, www.whale museum.org

12 English Camp (Bell Point, Mount Young)

WHAT TO EXPECT: Three short hikes exploring the history of English Camp, the quiet shoreline of Garrison Bay, and the spectacular views from the summit of Mount Young

GRADE: Easy to Bell Point and on the short interpretive loop. Moderate due to elevation gain to the summit of Mount Young.

APPROXIMATE LENGTH: 2-mile loop to Bell Point, 0.5-mile interpretive loop, 2 miles out and back to the summit of Mount Young

APPROXIMATE TIME: 3 hours for all three hikes

GETTING THERE: From the ferry terminal in Friday Harbor, follow Spring Street to Second Street and turn right. Second Street will turn into Guard Street. Turn right onto Tucker Avenue, which will turn into

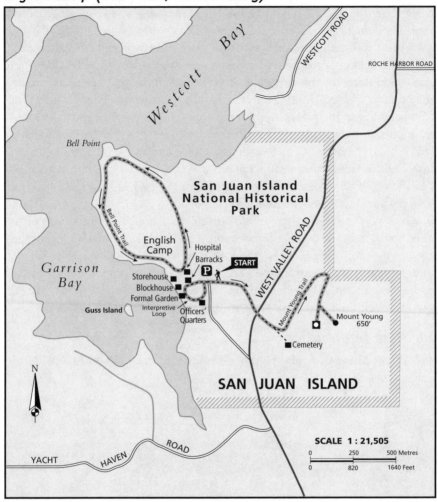

Roche Harbor Road. About 9 miles from Friday Harbor, turn left (south) toward English Camp onto West Valley Road. The entrance to the park will be on your right (west), approximately 1 mile from the intersection.

The Trail

There are actually three separate hikes you can do at English Camp, all short and easily doable with a few hours at the park. The first hike is a loop past the historic buildings and grounds, the second goes out to Bell Point, and the third is a short but steep walk to magnificent views atop Mount Young.

English Camp lies along tranquil and tree-sheltered Garrison Bay and, along with American Camp on the south end of San Juan Island, forms the San

Juan Island National Historical Park. Here you can explore the other site of the Pig War standoff on an easy 0.5-mile interpretive loop through historic English Camp. The camp includes a historic log blockhouse, storehouse, hospital, and barracks, as well as a small restored formal garden and Officers' Quarters site. The barracks and blockhouse are open to the public from June 1 through Labor Day, but are closed in the off-season.

More than just its Pig War history, excavations from the parade grounds show that English Camp was also an important site used by Native Americans from about A.D. 600 to as recently as the 1850s. Native Americans used the site to harvest and process camas and berries. Bones of salmon and herring have also been found in a large shell midden here, as have examples of bone, stone, and shells carved for personal adornment. In 1860 the Royal Marines moved large portions of the midden to fill in wetlands and create the spacious parade grounds seen by today's visitors. Wheelbarrow loads also were hauled to Officers' Hill, where terraces were constructed for officers' housing.

For bird lovers, English Camp is also a good birding spot, particularly in the spring when you may find osprey, bald eagles, flycatchers, swallows, wrens, kinglets, thrushes, vireos, warblers, tanagers, grosbeaks, and finches here. You may even spot or hear the gobble of wild turkeys.

The 2-mile round-trip to Bell Point starts at the east end of the parking lot and creates a level semiloop out to a picnic area on the point. Ignore a spur trail

View of English Camp and Garrison Bay, San Juan Island

Roche Harbor and Mitchell Hill Trails

Not to be overlooked are the several miles of trails that wind their way through Roche Harbor lands and the Washington Department of Natural Resource's Mitchell Hill area east of English Camp. Many of these trails, also used by mountain bikers and horse riders, are remnants of logging roads, and several remain unsigned and unmaintained, making it easy to get lost here. Local residents have been working with Roche Harbor Resort and the Department of Natural Resources to sign some of the main trails connecting with Mitchell Hill, Mount Young, and the main resort. Hiking maps are available at the resort's Hotel de Haro front desk, as well as from the San Juan Island Trails Committee's Web site at www.sanjuanislandtrails.org.

to the right shortly after the start, which leads out to the road. At 0.25 mile you'll stay straight ahead, ignoring yet another spur about 0.15 mile farther, and continue straight ahead out to the point. When finished admiring the view, simply continue around the point and meet up with the original trail you took in to retrace your steps to the parking lot.

The last hike, a short but stiff climb to the rocky ledges and grassy slopes of Mount Young, will reward you with some of the best views over the west side of San Juan Island and beyond. It's also a great spot to catch the sunset. You'll find the trail to Mount Young at the east end of the English Camp parking lot. Allow about an hour for the round-trip to the summit. The first stretch of trail climbs 0.25 mile through dense forest back to West Valley Road, where it crosses the road and then continues climbing past a gate on a dirt road.

In less than 0.5 mile, you'll reach a junction just after a switchback in the trail. Here, the right fork leads to a small cemetery where a handful of British marines lie buried, most ironically killed, as told by the stories on the headstones, during the twelve-year Pig War standoff by accidents rather than military conflict.

Take time to notice the Garry oak woodlands here, most commonly found on dry, rocky slopes on the San Juan Islands, along with Pacific madrone, bigleaf maple, and Douglas fir. These areas were once burned by Native Americans to maintain habitat for game animals and to grow plants such as camas for food and weaving. As is the case on American Camp's prairies, the National Park Service has been performing prescribed burns here since 1997 to maintain the oak woodland landscape, which would otherwise likely be taken over by Douglas firs in a process of forest succession. In spring you might also find the purple flowers of shooting stars here, along with fawn lilies and monkey flower.

To continue toward the summit, bear left at the junction and continue your climb. The trail climbs steadily and at times steeply as you make your way around the north side of the mountain, reaching your first views on the lower summit ledges at about 1 mile from the parking lot.

Here, the views over Garrison Bay and Haro Strait and on to Canada's Vancouver Island and Gulf Islands are spectacular. To the north lie Spieden and Sentinel Islands, along with Stuart Island. To the south lie the Olympic Peninsula and the glacier-carved summits of the Olympic Mountains. You can spend your time here watching the boats navigate the waters of Mosquito Pass and the numerous other bays and inlets below you.

From here, you can backtrack to the trail that continues climbing a short way to the rocky summit. Total elevation gain from the parking lot is approximately 590 feet.

From the summit, a trail descends down the northeast slopes of Mount Young, leading to an extensive trail system on Roche Harbor lands and connecting to a series of logging roads and trails on adjacent Department of Natural Resources property on Mitchell Hill. It's advisable, however, to only explore this area with a good map, as the network of trails can be very confusing. You'll simply retrace your steps back to the parking area.

Lopez Island

Of the three biggest islands in the San Juans, Lopez is probably least known for its hiking opportunities. With no large parks on the scale of Moran State Park or San Juan National Historical Park, hikes on Lopez are mainly short trips along the island's beautiful coastlines. The south shore of the island in particular, accessible by several short hikes, is among the most scenic spots in the islands.

13 Little Bird Trail, Big Tree Loop

WHAT TO EXPECT: Two short hikes through forest in Odlin County Park, passing large trees and views over Upright Channel

GRADE: Easy due to short distance and minimal elevation gain

APPROXIMATE LENGTH: A 1-mile loop for Big Tree Trail, 1.5 miles out and back for Little Bird Trail

APPROXIMATE TIME: 2 hours for both hikes

GETTING THERE: From the Lopez Island ferry landing, drive Ferry Road less than 1 mile and turn right into Odlin County Park. Trails start from the campground access road along the beach.

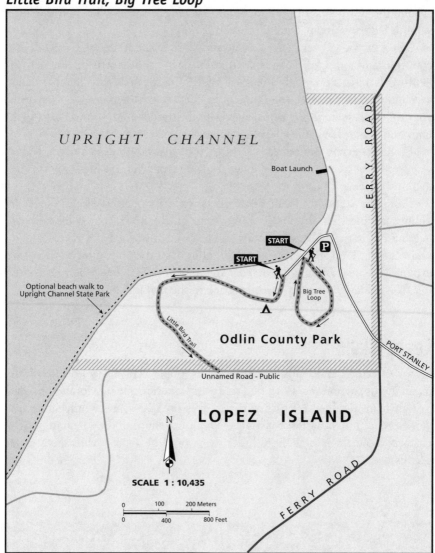

The Hike

While they're more short forest strolls than hikes, Odlin County Park never-theless has two short trails for visitors that can be completed within about an hour or two. Both originate along the gravel road accessing campsites and make for a good choice for campers at the park or for those spending a day or two exploring the island.

The aptly named Big Tree Trail, found next to campsite number 12, makes a short but pleasant loop through forest with some impressive Douglas fir and cedar trees. Several social side trails can be confusing here, but park staff have put together trail maps for the area. Look for maps at the trailhead, or check with the park office.

The second option is the Little Bird Trail, located farther west along the campsite access road toward the bluff-top campsites. This trail winds through forest and along the island's west-facing bluffs, with scenic views through the trees over Upright Channel toward Shaw Island. The trail ends at a publicly accessible road; here, you can either retrace your steps or turn left, walk the road to Ferry Road, and then re-enter the park through the main vehicular entrance. Total distance is approximately 1.5 miles.

Big Tree Trail, Lopez Island

While not an official "trail," yet a third and perhaps the most interesting option is to walk the beach, all publicly owned tidelands, from Odlin County Park south to Upright Channel State Park, a twenty-acre day-use area with picnic tables (some that have seen better days) and a sandy beach. It's a distance of approximately 2 miles that's best done at low to mean or average tide due to overhanging and downed trees along the route. At tides above about 5 feet, the walk, though not impossible, becomes much more difficult. Along this undeveloped section of shoreline, you can watch the ferries glide past on their way to and from Friday Harbor. By leaving a car at Upright Channel State Park, you'll avoid the need to retrace your steps; otherwise, it's a 2-mile walk back on the road or back along the beach.

For More Information

San Juan County Parks, (360) 378–8420, www.co.san-juan.wa.us/parks/lopez.html

WHAT TO EXPECT: A short hike through forest to the rocky south shoreline of Lopez Island, with abundant marine life and views over the turbulent waters of Cattle Pass

GRADE: Easy due to the short distance and minimal elevation gain

APPROXIMATE LENGTH: About 1 mile out and back

APPROXIMATE TIME: 1 hour

GETTING THERE: From the ferry landing, follow Ferry Road to Lopez Village and Fisherman Bay Road. Take Fisherman Bay Road for a mile and turn right onto Airport Road (look for the signs). Turn left from Airport Road onto Shark Reef Road after a short distance, and look for the trailhead at a small turnout with a bike rack on the right-hand side of the road.

The Hike

Shark Reef is one of the most popular spots on Lopez Island, and this short walk will take you out to this scenic overlook over Cattle Pass, where you can watch the harbor seals play in the lively current or haul out (climb out of the water) onto the rocks offshore. The short walk, less than a mile, winds its way through

Shark Reef Recreation Area shoreline, Lopez Island

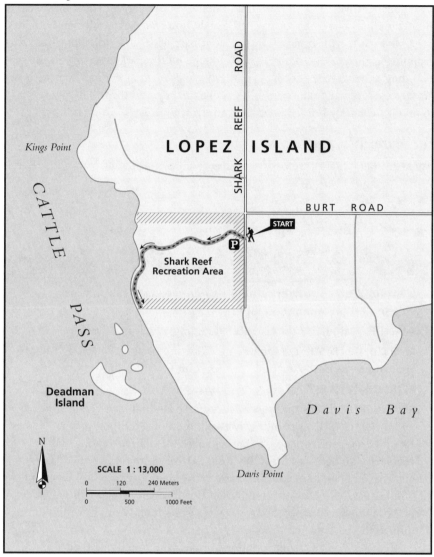

one of the last remaining old-growth forests on Lopez Island and makes a good stop on a bike ride around the island or as a destination in itself. Along the way, you might spot owls, woodpeckers, and bald eagles that nest in the area.

Upon reaching the shoreline, you'll look out on a sweeping view of San Juan Channel between Lopez and San Juan Islands. On a cloudless day the Olympics are clearly visible to the southwest. Some scrambling down the rocks takes you to the water and the kelp beds, rock formations, and tide pools prime for exploration. To watch the strong swirling currents of Cattle Pass, your best bet is to time your visit with an ebb (receding) tide, when the current flows most swiftly along the cliffs. The best time to see the seals, however, is typically between tides.

A well-worn path leads south to a spot parallel to some offshore rock outcroppings. Throughout the year, seals lounge on the rocks and play in the surrounding slow waters. Although you can typically spot wildlife here with the naked eye, you may find a pair of binoculars handy as well. When you're ready to move on, simply retrace your steps to the trailhead.

For More Information

San Juan County Parks, (360) 378–8420, www.co.san-juan.wa.us/parks/ lopez.html

15 Watmough Bay–Point Colville

WHAT TO EXPECT: Two short walks to a wild-feeling beach and rocky coastline on the south shore of Lopez Island

GRADE: Easy due to short distance and minimal elevation gain

APPROXIMATE LENGTH: Less than 1 mile out and back to Watmough Bay, approximately 1 mile out and back to Point Colville

APPROXIMATE TIME: 2 hours for both hikes

GETTING THERE: From the Lopez Island ferry landing, drive south for approximately 2.1 miles on Ferry Road, then turn left onto Center Road. Drive approximately 5.8 miles south on Center Road, which veers left and becomes Mud Bay Road. Drive south on Mud Bay Road approximately 4 miles and turn right onto Aleck Bay Road. In less than 1 mile, turn left onto Watmough Bay Road, which becomes dirt. Just before the END OF COUNTY ROAD sign, turn left and head downhill 0.25 mile to the parking area.

To reach Point Colville, continue driving the rough dirt road 0.3 mile beyond the END OF COUNTY ROAD sign, where you will find the trail on the right and parking on the left at a small turnout in the road.

The Hike

The far southeast corner of Lopez Island feels like a world away from the rest of the San Juans and is one of the least developed spots on the three biggest islands. Spared from the clearing of forest for farmland that much of the rest of Lopez Island has been subjected to, this corner offers two short but scenic hikes to explore a secluded beach and a wild, rocky shoreline.

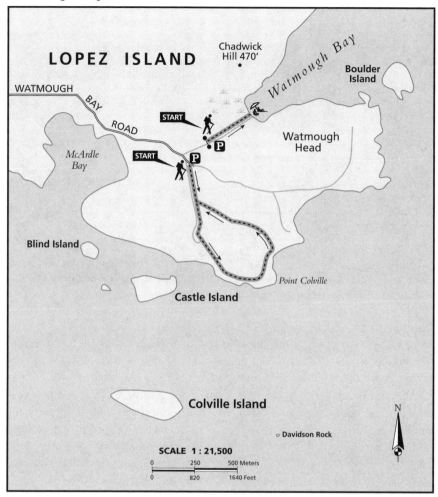

The first short walk to Watmough Bay crosses land protected in a partner-ship between the federal Bureau of Land Management (BLM) and the San Juan County Land Bank. Portions of the beach at Watmough Bay, along with a con-servation easement to protect the adjacent wetland, were a generous gift by the island's Oles family to the Land Bank in 1993.

This short walk along a gated gravel trail leads to a 70-foot stretch of pebble-and-sand beach cupped between rocky and forested hillsides. Along the way you'll pass the eight-acre cattail wetland protected to maintain the bay's ecosys-tem. The BLM manages the area as an Area of Critical Concern to protect its natural habitat. It's a perfect place to get away and contemplate life on a lonely beach. Please help protect this fragile place; trails are open to foot traffic only,

Watmough Bay, Lopez Island

and no fires or overnight camping are permitted. Dogs must be leashed to protect wildlife in the area.

Just down the road from Watmough Bay is spectacular Point Colville. During the nineteenth century, the U.S. Coast Guard withdrew tips and points of several of the larger San Juan Islands from the public domain for lighthouse and navigational purposes. But in 1976 the Coast Guard determined that all or parts of the withdrawals (like Point Colville) were no longer needed, returning those lands to be managed by the BLM. Today, through a combination of withdrawal lands, land exchanges, and purchases, BLM–administered lands total about 865 acres in the San Juans and are mainly managed as natural areas. Like Watmough Bay, while day use is allowed, you're asked to stay on existing trails and to respect the fragile nature of these lands.

Point Colville is accessed by a short walk through forest, leading to the wild, rocky south shore of Lopez Island. You'll find several plant communities in the area including meadow, bog, bluff, and intertidal areas. You'll walk through a forest of Douglas fir and white fir, along with alder, Pacific yew, Pacific madrone, wild rose, serviceberry, salmonberry, red flowering currant, ferns, and grasses. Trees here and at Iceberg Point to the west are well over 200 years old, among the last remaining virgin forest stands on Lopez Island.

Soon after beginning the hike, you'll reach a fork in the trail—bear right here, as you'll loop back on the left-trending trail. You'll break out of forest onto an open, rocky shoreline. Here, open grasses are interspersed with wild strawberry, wild rose, forbs, and lichens covering the exposed rock outcrops. Bracken fern and asters grow along the rocky shoreline. Just offshore is the rocky mound of Castle Island National Wildlife Refuge, with Colville Island and tiny Davidson Rock just a little farther offshore. Colville Island supports a nesting population of tufted puffins, one of the few places on Washington's inland waters these birds are found nesting.

Once you've had your fill of exploring, simply follow the trail east along the shoreline, where it shortly loops back into the forest, rejoining the main trail back to the trailhead.

For More Information

Bureau of Land Management, (509) 665–2100, www.or.blm.gov/spokane

16 Iceberg Point

WHAT TO EXPECT: Combine this trip with a kayak trip along the south shore of Lopez Island to hike 1 mile of windswept bluffs with expansive ocean views.

GRADE: Easy due to short distance and minimal elevation gain

APPROXIMATE LENGTH: 2 miles out and back from Iceberg Point east to Flint Beach

APPROXIMATE TIME: 1 hour

GETTING THERE: Unfortunately, at this point the only entirely legal way to access this spectacular area is by boat, either launching from Mac-Kaye Harbor or from Agate Beach, as there is presently no legal public access over land to the site. To get to MacKaye Harbor from the Lopez Island ferry landing, drive south on Ferry Road for 2.1 miles and turn left onto Center Road. After 5.8 miles, Center Road turns into Mud Bay Road. Drive Mud Bay Road 3 miles and turn right onto MacKaye Harbor Road. Turn quickly right and follow this road to its end at the MacKaye Harbor boat ramp. Parking is available on the small hill just above the ramp. After kayaking you'll find a small beach at the north end of the small cove just north of Iceberg Point, with a primitive trail scrambling up the bluffs.

The Bureau of Land Management is currently attempting to acquire a walking easement to the area from the road's end just south of Agate Beach, but as of now, land access is only possible by permission from the landowner. Please respect the private property rights in this area.

Iceberg Point

The Hike

Iceberg Point, owned and maintained as an Area of Critical Concern by the Bureau of Land Management, contains some of the most spectacular landscape on Lopez Island, encompassing the open, rugged bluffs and rocky coast of the south shore of the island. Until an overland access point can be secured, your best bet for exploring this area is by kayak. You'll find a small pebble beach on the north side of a small cove just north of Iceberg Point and its channel marker for landing.

From the beach, a primitive trail scrambles steeply up the bluff, where you'll find a trail through open forest south to the open bluffs. Here, primitive trails wind their way east along the bluffs, allowing you to wander as long as you wish. Gaze over the wild south coast of Lopez, where extensive areas of bull kelp below the rugged cliffs provide habitat for a variety of marine life, seals play on the rocks offshore, and, in season, you may spot orca whales as they feed on salmon migrating through Rosario Strait. More than one hundred species of birds also inhabit the area, including grebes, cormorants, gulls, waterfowl, guillemots, scooters, terns, auklets, murres, oystercatchers, and other assorted shorebirds.

A fairly well-defined trail follows the top of the shoreline bluffs east to a high point and a concrete monument that serves as a reference point for the

U.S.-Canada border farther to the north. You're free to wander along this trail, which eventually ends in about 1 mile with a view over Flint Beach. Simply retrace your steps when finished. The entire area is designated for day use only and is a sensitive area, so it's best to stay on trails to avoid further damaging this fragile landscape.

For More Information

Bureau of Land Management, (509) 665–2100, www.or.blm.gov/spokane/

U.S.-Canada monument at Iceberg Point, Lopez Island

WHAT TO EXPECT: A short hike to explore the tide pools and marshes around this interesting spit on the east side of Lopez Island

GRADE: Easy due to short distance and minimal elevation gain

APPROXIMATE LENGTH: 2 miles out and back

APPROXIMATE TIME: 1 hour

GETTING THERE: From the Lopez Island ferry landing, follow Ferry Road and turn left onto Center Road after about 2.1 miles. Turn left again after 0.7 mile onto Cross Road, then right after 0.5 mile onto Port Stanley Road. Turn quickly left again at Bakerview Road, following the road straight into the park.

The Hike

More known for its camping than hiking trails, Spencer Spit nevertheless makes a rewarding stop if you're looking for a short walk on Lopez and the chance to explore along the shoreline around the spit, and among the driftwood along the mile-long sandy beach. In total, you'll find about 2 miles of trail here leading around the camping and picnic area up on the bluffs down to and along the beach.

Slough at Spencer Spit, Lopez Island

Spencer Spit State Park

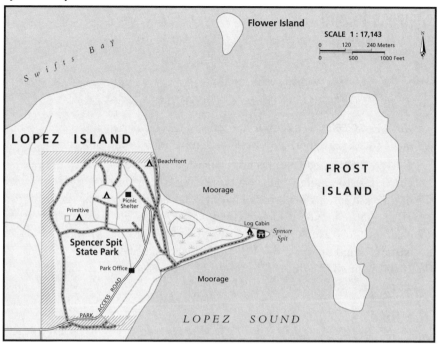

The Spencer family, after which the spit and park are named, are a well-known name around Lopez Island, farming on the island since 1886 on 160 acres near the present-day park. The stone cellar of the old Spencer house can be seen near the spit, with a replica of the original log cabin built by the Spencers located near the tip of the spit.

Spencer Spit is an example of a sand spit enclosing a saltchuck lagoon, formed over a long period of time by the action of wind and tide. The spit itself is a narrow neck of land that nearly connects Lopez and tiny privately owned Frost Island. Clam digging and crabbing are popular along the spit, but check local regulations and red tide warnings first. Bird-watchers will find interesting the many shorebirds that inhabit the area.

For More Information

Washington State Parks, (360) 902–8844, www.parks.wa.gov

Cypress Island

The Trails of Cypress Island

WHAT TO EXPECT: Over 20 miles of trails to spectacular cliff tops and quiet coves, past ponds and wetlands, and among beautiful forests

GETTING THERE: Since there is no regular ferry service to Cypress Island, you'll have to arrange your own transportation. From Anacortes, one of the best options is a private charter. You can arrange to be dropped off and picked up by Paraclete Charters (800–808–2999, www.paraclete charters.com), which runs daily trips to destinations throughout the islands. Island Sherpa (360–202–1282, www.islandsherpa.com) and Island Express Charters (877–473–9777, www.islandexpresscharters .com) offer similar service.

The Hike

Cypress Island, while not considered by some to be part of the main San Juan Islands group, is nonetheless a very worthwhile destination for any hiker looking to explore one of the wildest islands in the region. Unlike San Juan, Orcas, or Lopez Island, Cypress is a look back into the past, before the islands were forever changed by the wave of development. Cypress escaped heavy development due to its difficult access, rugged terrain, and poor soils for farming. Today only about 10 percent of the 5,500-acre island is developed, the rest being owned and managed by the Washington Department of Natural Resources as a natural-area preserve, or as a natural-resources conservation area to protect resources and provide for low-impact recreation. The island's trails are open to hikers only—pets must remain leashed and are not permitted on the Cypress Lake or Eagle Cliff Trails, to protect wildlife. Trail maps and natural-area brochures on current public-use restrictions are available from the department.

You'll find lowland forests, quiet sand and cobble beaches, grassy balds, miles of trail, ocean views, and spectacular ponds and wetlands here. Forests of Douglas fir, western red cedar, and western hemlock blanket the island, along with grand fir, shore pine, Sitka spruce, and Pacific yew. Pacific madrone and Rocky Mountain juniper are found on drier slopes, along with Idaho fescue, camas, and colorful paintbrush.

A network of about 20 miles of trails covers the island, many of them following remnant primitive roads past twisted cables and log piles left from the days of timber harvesting on the island. It's not possible to explore the whole place in one day, so allow yourself ample time with an overnight camping trip.

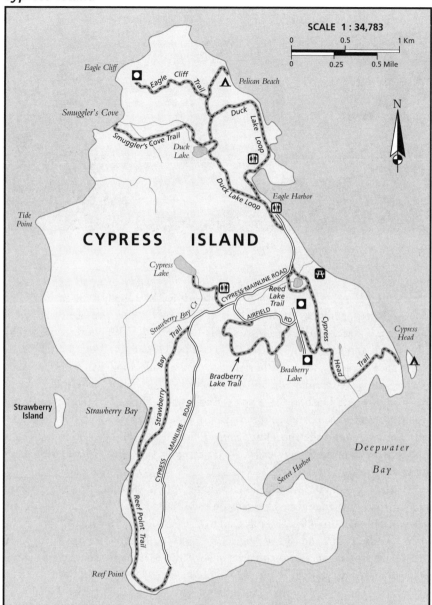

SCALE 1 : 34,783

From waterfront camps at Pelican Beach on the northeast side of the island, the 2.6-mile out-and-back hike to Eagle Cliff is among the most spectacular hikes on Cypress. Climbing moderately from the beach through Douglas fir and western red cedar with a lush understory of sword fern, the trail breaks out of the forest after about 1 mile and scrambles over rocky ledges to the cliff, where you'll find jaw-dropping views down to Rosario Strait below you, across

View from trail to Eagle Cliff, Cypress Island

Obstruction Pass and Orcas Island, and south to the Olympic Peninsula. The trail is closed seasonally from February 1 to July 15 to protect threatened, endangered, and sensitive species. Staying on the trail will help to protect sensitive forest and the fragile soils of the grass-bald habitat.

From Pelican Beach, another moderate 2.8-mile loop will take you past Duck Lake, a spectacular wetland for bird-watchers, and on to Eagle Cove at the head of Eagle Harbor. Here you'll find a quiet, sheltered, pebble-and-sand beach, where you can listen to the chatter of kingfishers, or watch herons gracefully foraging along the shoreline. From Duck Lake, you can also hike the 2.4 miles out and back to Smuggler's Cove on the west side of the island, with views out over Rosario Strait.

South of Eagle Harbor, the 4-mile-long Cypress Mainline Road, a remnant logging road, provides access to trails on the south side of the island. Along the way you can take the 0.5-mile spur trail to Cypress Lake, the largest lake on the island. At the south end of the Mainline Road, the Reef Point and Strawberry Bay Trails provide access to the west side of the island. Please respect private property here and stay on the trail.

If you're camped at Cypress Head, the steep climb up the Cypress Head Trail from the beach will give you access to tiny Reed Lake, a total of 2.1 miles from Cypress Head. Or hike the 2.2 miles following the Airfield Road trail to the airfield for outstanding views to the north and southeast, and to Bradberry Lake.

For More Information

Washington State Department of Natural Resources, Northwest Region, Sedro-Woolley, Washington, (360) 856–3500

More Guided Hikes

Another great way to get to know more about the San Juan Islands is on a guided interpretive walk. In addition to walks sponsored by park rangers, the following groups have regular classes and walks through which you'll learn about geology, wildlife, plant life, and other topics.

- San Juan Nature Institute (360–378–3646, www.sjnature.org) offers a selection of courses and lectures in an outdoor classroom setting. Instructors come from a variety of backgrounds and teach on a variety of subjects from otters to insects. Many of the classes are taught on San Juan Island, with a few classes also held on Lopez or Orcas Islands.

- San Juan Islands Audubon Society (www.sjiaudubon.org) offers bird walks monthly on one of the four islands in the San Juan Islands serviced by the ferry system. The public is free to join them.

- Skylark Nature Tours (360–378–3068, skylark@rockisland.com) also offers birding, natural-history, and human-history tours in the islands, teaching about whole ecosystems.

Duck Lake, Cypress Island

Chapter 3:
Exploring the Water

Touring the San Juans by kayak or boat is one of the best ways to experience the serene beauty of the islands. With more than 400 miles of shoreline to explore, the San Juans have become one of the top kayaking destinations in the country. The opportunities are seemingly endless, from quiet coves and current-filled passes to open bays and straits.

There's also no better way to experience the wonders of the diverse marine life in the San Juans than by kayak. It's not uncommon to have a curious seal approach you for a closer look, and you'll be able to observe the abundant shorebird life found around the islands. And there's little that's more exhilarating than spotting orca whales or porpoises from the intimacy of a kayak. Paddling along the islands' shorelines, you can also discover large purple and scarlet sea stars, forests of bull kelp swaying in the current, and anemones ranging in color from pink to orange and brown.

It's no understatement to say that kayaking has surged in popularity in the San Juans—perhaps among the best measures is the proliferation of shops and guides that now cater to visitors. Guide services in the islands were virtually nonexistent twenty-five years ago, but today over a dozen outfitters offer everything from kayak rentals and equipment to a variety of trips, from half-day paddles to several-day multisport excursions.

Of course, the San Juan Islands are also among the most popular boating and sailing destinations in the country. If you're sailing or yachting to the San Juans on your own, you'll find marinas and moorage at state parks, town harbors, and throughout the smaller outer islands. For those without their own boats or with less experience, you'll find both skippered and bareboat charters of all types for rent. A list of charters available around the islands is provided at the end of this chapter.

When to Go

Kayaking and boating in the San Juans can be enjoyed year-round, although with the longer days, warmer temperatures, and calmer weather, it's easy to understand why summer is the most popular season. Calmer and sunnier summer conditions in the San Juans typically start appearing in April and can persist through September and even into early October. During this time, temperatures are cool to warm during the day, southerly winds prevail, and gale-force winds and storms are less frequent. Strong winds can, however, develop in the summertime, particularly during hot days when heating and rising air over the mainland draws westerly winds off the cooler ocean through the Strait of Juan de Fuca. Under these conditions, twenty-five-knot afternoon winds are not uncommon and can create treacherous boating and paddling conditions. On days predicted to be warm, you'll usually encounter the calmest winds in the morning before land heating occurs and in the evening when winds subside. Thick fogs can blanket the islands in later summer months and may not burn off in some locations until late afternoon.

Adding to the meteorological complexity is the rugged terrain, making local conditions highly variable. Boaters may experience calm conditions in one area, only to find rough seas by simply rounding a point of land. Narrow passes between islands may compress and funnel winds, also creating locally rough conditions on nearby waters.

In fall, winter, and early spring, weather becomes much less predictable in the San Juans. Storms bring with them strong winds, typically from the south but possibly from all directions, along with the potential for heavy rains. A few times every winter, arctic fronts drop south from Canada, bringing cold temperatures, occasional snow, and strong north winds. If you do decide to venture out in the off-season, anticipate the very real possibility of rapidly changing conditions. While you'll find much less boat traffic and more open campsites, wind storms and rain squalls can sweep in rapidly off the water, and with the shorter days you'll have to seriously consider how far you can realistically paddle each day. Many beaches also develop steeper profiles in winter, making launching and landing more difficult. If you're on an extended trip, it's much more likely that you'll need contingency plans in the event that rough seas, fog, or other weather conditions make paddling impossible.

Marine Traffic

In a popular boating area like the San Juans, you'll have plenty of company on the water, most notably during the peak boating season in summer. As much as weather and currents can affect your travels, boat traffic is also another major factor to consider.

This is particularly true for kayakers. With such a low profile to the water, kayaks can be very hard for boaters to spot, especially larger barges and boats, even more so when seas are choppy or kayakers are traveling alone or in small groups. Never assume that a boater can see you—always remain on the defensive for oncoming boats, and be aware that larger ferries, tugs, and freighters have limited maneuvering ability and may travel at speeds of up to twenty knots. If you're in a group, paddle closely together to make the group more visible. As a rule of thumb, gauge the angle of your bow with the ship's bow, and never attempt to cross a shipping lane unless you're sure you can successfully

Sea-Kayaking Safety

To the inexperienced, sea kayaking in the San Juans may seem like a fairly safe, benign sport. And while on most occasions paddling will be a peaceful experience, its potential dangers should not be underestimated. Without proper planning and an ability to read the conditions around you, a kayak trip can quickly turn from relaxing to harrowing. Tidal currents around the San Juan Islands are strong, and, combined with the area's changeable weather and varied topography, rough seas and tide rips can create hazardous paddling conditions. Kayakers have capsized by misjudging tide rips, or have been swept well off-course and into dangerous conditions by failing to consider the currents along their route. In fact, there have even been a handful of kayaking fatalities around the islands.

Prior to embarking on any trip away from shore and out of protected waters, you should know how to read tide and current charts, be aware of weather conditions, be comfortable with turning and bracing in rough water, and know how to perform an open-water rescue. Water temperatures generally range between forty-six and fifty-six degrees, and air temperatures over the water are often significantly cooler than land temperatures. If capsized, you may have less than thirty minutes to get yourself or a paddling partner out of the water before hypothermia sets in. Only the most expert of paddlers should ever venture out alone.

Fortunately for less experienced paddlers, there is now a wide range of guided kayak trips to choose from in the islands. Most of today's guided trips use relatively stable double kayaks; many trips require no prior paddling experience. They're a good option for those who want to venture out on a longer excursion into more exposed and open waters in the relative safety of a guided tour.

complete the crossing. Shipping lanes in major straits in the San Juans are marked in red or purple on navigation charts.

Even when they can see you, some boaters seem unaware of the difficulties that they may pose to kayakers. Even when not in the direct path of a passing boat, unanticipated boat wakes, even from far-off passing barges, can easily flip an unprepared kayaker, especially combined with tide rips. Keep an eye out for approaching wakes, and turn into the wake when you can to avoid from being hit broadside.

Understanding Currents and Tides

No kayaker should venture out in the San Juans on his or her own without a good understanding of currents and tides. Tides in the Pacific Northwest are highly dynamic, having two high and two low periods daily—commonly referred to as the "higher high" and "lower low"—along with high and low tides. The typical tidal range in the San Juans is about 10 feet, with the greatest tidal exchanges occurring during full or new moons.

Given such a significant tidal exchange and the varied topography of the San Juans, it's not surprising to find strong currents here. Currents in the islands depend greatly on local geography and specific tidal conditions, but can vary in speed from one knot (a weak current that will slow your forward progress) up to seven knots (a strong current that you can't paddle against).

The interaction of currents with local topography often forms tide "rips," eddies, boils, and other turbulent water features. Tide rips are common throughout the San Juans and are distinguished by waves with a seemingly erratic, "confused" pattern, or by a low roar from a distance. You may encounter them where two currents intersect, or where shallow waters, bends in channels, or points of land alter the current's flow. When paddling in such conditions, it's often difficult to find balance or anticipate the water's motion. Waves created by tide rips can be made significantly more treacherous by boat traffic, or by winds blowing opposite to the current's direction. While some of the more notable tide rips in the San Juans are shown on maps and navigation charts, many others are simply too complex to consider with regularity. If you're planning a stop into one of the many kayak shops around the islands to rent or purchase equipment for your trip, local guides are often willing to share their knowledge of local conditions.

Kayakers in the San Juans can reference several documents, charts, and information resources to help with trip planning. The National Oceanic and Atmospheric Administration publishes annual tide tables, predicting tidal changes for much of the Pacific Ocean. Similarly, the Canadian Hydrographic Service publishes its own tables, also good for one year. Current tables and charts are a good information source, as they'll help you predict the strength and direction of currents for a given tide. The University of South Carolina (http://tbone.biol.sc.edu/tide/sites_uswest.html) provides an online resource for tides and currents at various locations around the San Juan Islands. Many state parks throughout the islands post tide changes at marine campsites or launch points. Finally, nautical charts showing topography and bathymetry are also a valuable tool to understand how wind and current can locally increase or decrease in velocity in certain locations. A good source for nautical charts is Sea Trails Marine Maps (www.seatrails.com).

One caution about current and tide charts and tables. They're meant to be guides, and their predictions of changes are just that—predictions that can be highly variable based on local conditions. You may find, for example, the current in your area flowing opposite to what's predicted on the tide chart, or that the predicted "slack" time never really materializes. Under these circumstances, good kayakers will always keep acutely aware of local conditions.

Speed and Distance

For kayakers, determining how far you can paddle in a day is not as easy as it may seem. Even for strong paddlers, speed and distance often have more to do with weather and currents than paddling strength. As a very general rule, given minimal current or wind, a paddling speed of two to two and one-half knots per hour (one knot is one nautical mile per hour) is considered a good pace for a beginner, with three knots being a brisk but comfortable paddling pace.

Ask kayakers around the islands and they'll generally tell you that one might cover 12 nautical miles a day (about 1.1 land miles) during a moderate paddle, while experienced paddlers may comfortably cover 20 miles in a day. But with currents of two and a half knots or more fairly common around the islands, you may find yourself making little headway if paddling against the current. Similarly, while winds less than ten knots seldom cause paddling trouble, you'll find yourself hard-pressed to make progress by paddling into winds twenty knots or more. Going with the current and wind can be quite another story—with the wind and current in your favor, you may be able to double your speed to over five knots per hour!

What to Bring

Having the right equipment and clothing can make or break a kayak trip in the San Juans. Not only should you prepare for potentially cold weather and constantly cold water, it's important to take seriously the various items that you'll need for an open-water rescue or other emergencies.

The "ten essentials" list for hikers in chapter 2 is a good starting point for what to bring on any kayak trip. The items on the list—which include sun protection, water, food, clothing, and other items—are equally important on any paddle trip. Many others, such as flotation devices and signals, are required by the U.S. government. If you're heading out on a guided trip, the company will typically provide this equipment:

- U.S. Coast Guard–approved personal flotation device
- paddle and paddle leash
- spray skirt
- bilge pump with flotation
- self-rescue paddle float
- whistle or air horn
- 50 feet of floating tow rope
- waterproof flashlight or chemical light stick
- repair kit (duct tape)

Access for All

For all that the San Juans have to offer paddlers and boaters, finding suitable launches and take-out points can sometimes be the biggest challenge. Longtime residents and visitors to the islands who remember the days of undeveloped shorelines in the 1950s and 1960s lament the loss of waterfront to private development. And, as recreation increases in popularity, clashes between landowners and boaters have increased. Exacerbating access difficulties is the fact that many of the steep, rocky shorelines along the islands simply aren't good places to haul out a boat or kayak.

The news, however, is not all bad. Thanks to a handful of farsighted souls who saw the approaching wave of development, boaters can enjoy the Cascadia Marine Trail, a network of public take-out locations and campsites throughout Puget Sound. The trail, ten years old in 2003 and stewarded by the Washington Water Trails Association, provides safe campsites for those traveling in small human- and wind-powered boats. Fees vary by site—camps on Cypress and Strawberry Islands are free. Camps are first-come, first-served and moorage is limited to three consecutive nights. Be aware that some of the camps can be quite crowded on more popular islands in summer. See the Washington Water Trails Association's Web site at www.wwta.org/trails for more information and for a copy of their helpful *Cascadia Marine Trail Guidebook,* available with an association membership.

Also unknown to many boaters is the fact that over three-quarters of the tidelands in the San Juan Islands below the ordinary high-water mark are in public ownership, meaning that you have a legal right to land on these tidelands. Be aware, however, that most public tidelands are not posted as such, and that this legal access is far from understood or embraced by many local landowners. A good source for locating public tidelands is the Great Pacific Recreation and Travel Map for the San Juan Islands (www.greatpacificmaps.com).

- waterproof drybags for extra clothing
- flotation at both ends of the kayak

Hypothermia is the single most imminent threat to kayakers in the San Juans. While it's a serious threat from tipping over, you can also rapidly lose body heat even while in your boat if you're exposed to any combination of wind, spray, or rain. To prepare yourself for potentially cold, wet conditions, bring along layers that will insulate you, even when wet, including polypropylene or wool. Avoid cotton, which might seem fine on a dry, hot day but will actually pull heat away from your body when wet.

Many experienced kayakers and guides in the islands also carry VHF radios, which broadcast periodic summaries of local weather conditions and forecasts for various points throughout the San Juan Islands and surrounding area.

Snapshot of the Trips

The San Juan Islands have something to offer all levels of boater and kayaker, from the complete novice seeking out a guided afternoon paddle to the adventurer looking for a multiday excursion. The trips in this book are only intended as suggestions—most can be done in a day or on an overnight trip, and many are listed here either because they are protected enough for less experienced paddlers or because they are one of the many trips offered by local guides. But certainly one of the greatest joys of kayaking is being able to explore wherever your curiosity takes you. Experienced boaters and paddlers often take longer trips on their own, visiting many of the larger islands and marine state parks as part of longer multiday excursions. Boaters and sailors visiting the islands will find a similar freedom and flexibility to explore the islands, with moorage available around the main islands as well as at many of the smaller state marine parks and private islands.

Depending on weather and currents, many kayak guides provide longer, multiday trips to destinations throughout the San Juan Islands. Where guided trips are offered, they are listed as options for each trip in this chapter, while you'll find a more complete list of kayak guides and outfitters at the end of the chapter. Charter companies also are increasingly teaming up with kayak guides and outfitters to offer "multisport" trips in the islands. Some will take you to the outer islands, where you can hike, kayak, or even mountain bike for the day and return to the main islands or the comfort of your boat.

Some of the more popular guided day trips are offered around **Roche Harbor–Westcott Bay** (Trip 7) on San Juan Island, along the **West Side of San Juan Island** (Trip 6), or out to **Jones Island** (Trip 1) or around **Obstruction Pass** (Trip 2) on Orcas Island. If you're looking to get out on your own for an easy to moderate paddle, **Griffin Bay** (Trip 5) on San Juan Island and **Shaw Island** (Trip 9) from Lopez Island offer two trips where you'll find generally weak currents but lots of scenery. If you're looking to get away from the crowds for a day's worth of paddling, the **Lopez Island's South Shore** (Trip 11) offers rugged scenery and abundant wildlife.

Experienced paddlers should consider a trip to **Stuart Island** (Trip 8) from San Juan Island, **James Island** (Trip 10) from Lopez, **Sucia Island** (Trip 4) or **Clark Island** (Trip 3) from Orcas, or around **Cypress Island** (Trip 12). Not only do these destinations offer more challenging currents and open-water crossings, they'll reward you with some of the rich natural and cultural history of the islands. Guided trips are offered for these destinations as well.

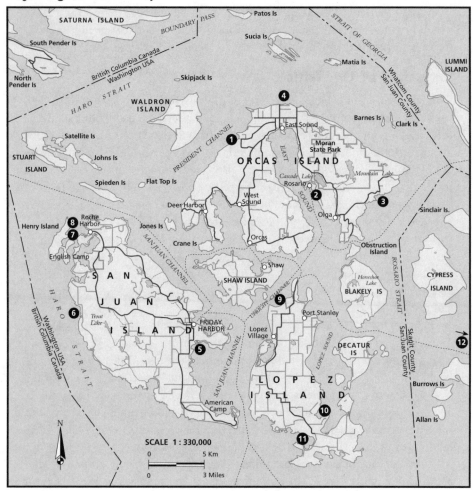

Orcas Island

Orcas Island offers a wide range of kayaking opportunities and serves as the launching point for many trips out to the northern state park islands of Clark, Sucia, Matia, and Patos. Around Orcas itself you'll find narrow passes, quiet harbors, and rugged shoreline fronting open straits. Compared to the other large islands, the 4-mile-long West Sound and 8-mile-long East Sound offer more water protected from currents for paddling, although winds can create rough conditions, particularly on East Sound. One of the few frustrations of paddling around Orcas is the relative lack of shoreline access compared to the other main islands.

If you're arriving on Orcas by boat, you'll find a number of moorage opportunities around the island. Guest moorage is available at West Sound, Olga, West Beach, Deer Harbor, and Rosario Resort. Some limited moorage is also available at Orcas Landing near the ferry dock. Many of the state parks and recreation areas on and around Orcas also offer mooring buoys on a first-come, first-served basis, with a maximum stay of three days, including Obstruction Pass on Orcas Island (two buoys), Patos Island (two buoys), Sucia Island (forty-eight buoys), Matia Island (two buoys), and Clark Island (seven buoys). Jones Island has seven buoys, along with a dock and twelve moorage floats. Many of these sites fill up during the peak summer season, particularly on weekends.

Unfortunately, kayakers wishing to walk on the ferry will not find any launching access at the Orcas ferry landing. Drivers with kayaks and other hand-carried boats can launch at the county road's end at West Beach, at the county dock west of West Sound Marina, and at North Beach, Doe Bay, Olga, Crescent Beach, and Obstruction Pass. Hand-carried boats can also be launched for a small fee at Deer Harbor, Rosario Resort, and Bartwood Lodge on Orcas Island's north shore.

1 West Beach–Jones Island–Wasp Islands

WHAT TO EXPECT: A moderate paddle down the rocky, forested west side of Orcas Island to a popular state marine park and through a handful of small scenic islands

LENGTH: Approximately 12 miles from West Beach to West Sound

DIFFICULTY: Moderate, with some moderate currents and short open-water crossings

GETTING THERE: From the Orcas Island ferry terminal, drive north on Orcas Road (Horseshoe Highway) approximately 0.75 mile past the town of East Sound. Turn left onto Enchanted Forest Road and drive 2.5 miles to the intersection of Enchanted Forest Road and West Beach Road. Continue straight through the intersection, finding West Beach at the end of the county road. While parking at the road's end is very limited, the adjacent West Beach Resort provides vehicle parking for $5.00 a night.

The Trip

This trip from West Beach makes a scenic full-day paddle that will take you to both the rugged western side of Orcas Island and to the beautiful Wasp Islands. On the way you'll pass Jones Island State Marine Park, one of the most popular

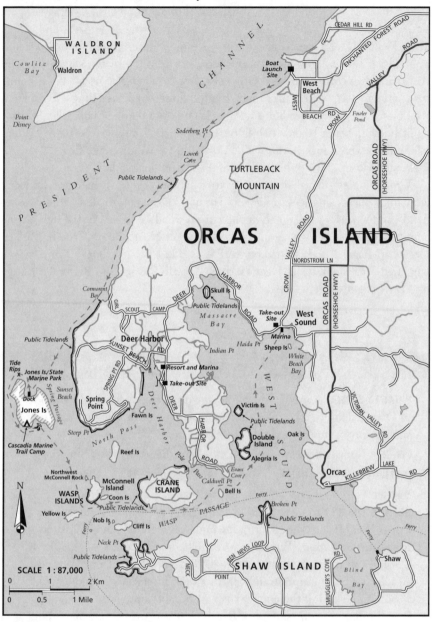

island parks in the San Juans, and a worthwhile diversion on its own for both kayakers and other boaters.

West Beach Resort on the northwest side of Orcas Island is a good launching site for kayakers heading about 2 nautical miles north to the Point Doughty

Recreation Site, which is only accessible to the public from the water, and for paddlers heading south toward Jones Island and the Wasp Islands. The resort charges a small fee ($10) for kayakers coming to launch on their own. Point Doughty is one of the least-used Cascadia Marine Trail campsites and a popular spot for divers, although paddlers will have to contend with tide rips that regularly form around the point.

If you're planning to head south from West Beach, time your trip with the south-flowing ebb current. Keep in mind that currents in President Channel can be quite strong, so your best option is to stay close to shore where currents are generally the weakest. The forested western side of Orcas Island offers rugged scenery, with numerous small coves and bays to explore. Along the way you'll pass Lovers Cove, where you'll find a small sea cave. On a favorable current, you can reach the southern tip of Orcas Island and Spring Passage in a few hours.

From here it's just a short paddle across Spring Passage to the north side of Jones Island. Beware of boat traffic when crossing this channel. Tide rips can also form off the north tip of Jones Island.

Jones Island is a gem of a state park, offering two good harbors, one on the north and one on the south side of the island, along with several pebbly beaches. The forested center of the island, reachable by a north-south trail connecting both harbors, is home to the island's notoriously tame deer. Hard as it may be to resist their cute gaze, not only is feeding them bad for their health, it's against the law.

Being only 0.5 mile from the southwest tip of Orcas Island, Jones Island is also easily accessible by boat, making the north harbor in particular a popular place during the summer. Luckily for kayakers, the island is part of the Cascadia Marine Trail, and you'll find the designated water trail site with room for about four tents on its southwest side. Other camps are located near the harbors on the north and south sides of the island. Potable water is available from April through September.

From Jones Island, you can continue your trip through the Wasp Islands, or shorten it by paddling east through North Pass, past Fawn Island, and into Deer Harbor where you can arrange a car shuttle to take out at the Deer Harbor Marina. If you choose to continue your trip, it's a relatively straightforward paddle across to the Wasp Islands, where you'll pass tiny Northwest McConnell Rock, a designated state park, and the larger McConnell Island, connected to the state park by a small land bridge at low tide.

You'll also pass scenic Yellow Island, easily picked out by its drier habitat and grassy slopes, which stand in stark contrast to the surrounding forested islands. Owned and managed by The Nature Conservancy, the eleven-acre island is a delight in spring when many of its over fifty species of wildflowers burst into bloom. The island also provides suitable habitat for the prickly pear, Washington State's only endemic species of cactus. Visitors approaching by boat can

Kayakers on Jones Island

land at the beach on the southeast side of the island below Dodd cabin. Two trail loops are open to the public year-round, from 10:00 A.M. to 4:00 P.M.

Narrow Wasp Passage, between Crane and Shaw Islands, can offer some protection during rough conditions as you paddle past the impressive waterside homes here. However, be aware that you're on the route of the Washington State Ferries, and stay close to shore and out of the main ferry navigation channel. The current here flows west on flood tides.

From here, you'll paddle past tiny Bell Island and north and east into Orcas Island's West Sound, passing Alegria and Double Islands (both with public tidelands) at its mouth. Note that currents are strong through Pole Pass to the west, between Crane and Orcas Island.

From here, it's approximately another 2 nautical miles of paddling to the San Juan County dock located west of West Sound Marina. Here, you'll find a pebbly beach just west of the dock that makes for a good take-out spot. Those with a little extra time and energy might want to explore pretty Skull Island State Park in Massacre Bay near the head of West Sound. It was here that one hundred Lummi Indians were reportedly massacred on the beach by a savage, slave-hunting northern tribe, leading to the series of rather macabre names for this area of West Sound.

Diving in the San Juan Islands

This book wouldn't be complete without some mention of the wonderful diving opportunities in the San Juans, among the best cold-water diving areas in the world. The cold waters and strong currents support a diverse array of marine plants and animals, and below the surface you'll find an amazing diversity of marine life, including orange, white, and crimson anemones, sea urchins, sea sponges, multicolored clown shrimp, rockfish, box crabs, kelp, and finger and cloud sponges. You may even spot a giant Pacific octopus, a wolf eel, or a giant ling cod.

There are literally hundreds of dive sites throughout the islands, ranging in all levels from beginning dives to the more advanced in areas where currents are stronger and there are steep walls.

If you're looking for a guided dive experience, Island Dive and Water Sports (800–303–8386, www.divesanjuan.com) offers single- and multiday trips, along with rental of equipment. The company offers dive trips year-round.

For More Information

Orcas Island–based Shearwater Adventures (360–376–4699, www.shearwater kayaks.com), located in East Sound, offers guided day trips along the west side of Orcas Island and through the Wasp Islands.

Jones Island State Marine Park, (360) 378–2044, www.parks.wa.gov/ moorage/parks/ m_008.asp

West Beach Resort (360–376–2240, www.westbeachresort.com) also offers guided afternoon and sunset kayak tours in summer.

2 East Sound–Obstruction Pass–Doe Island

WHAT TO EXPECT: A trip from the protected waters of East Sound, past a scenic state park beach, through narrow Obstruction Pass, and along the southeast shore of Orcas Island

LENGTH: Approximately 5 miles from Rosario Resort to Doe Bay Resort

DIFFICULTY: Moderate due to strong current in Obstruction Pass

GETTING THERE: To launch from Rosario Resort, turn left after exiting the ferry and drive Orcas Road (Horseshoe Highway) 7 miles, bearing

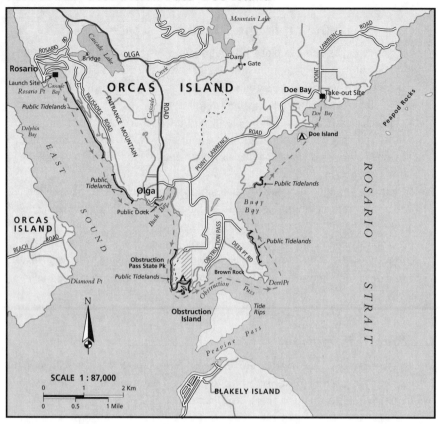

right at a signed junction toward Moran State Park and the village of East Sound. Continue straight ahead past Crescent Beach, then turn right onto Olga Road. At 14 miles from the ferry dock, turn right onto Rosario Road just before the entrance to Moran State Park and drive 1 mile. Kayaks can be launched from the beach near the marina.

The Trip

The area stretching from the eastern shore of East Sound to Doe Bay offers scenic shoreline, some challenging currents, coves for exploration, and the opportunity to see abundant wildlife. The numerous opportunities for launching or taking out kayaks at Rosario Resort, the tiny village of Olga, Obstruction Pass, or Doe Bay also add quite a bit of flexibility to your trip, meaning that you can tailor it to both the paddling conditions and your energy level. It's about 2.5 miles from Rosario Resort south and east to Obstruction Pass, and another 2.5 miles from Obstruction Pass to Doe Bay.

If you start your trip at Rosario, your first 2 miles of paddling will take you south along the east shore of East Sound. Currents here are generally weak, although northwest winds blowing over the shoulder of Mount Constitution can occasionally create rough paddling conditions. You'll reach Olga State Marine Park in 1.5 miles, where you'll find a dock at this small hamlet. The quiet shallow cove just east of here, in Buck Bay, supports an active shellfish-growing operation.

Continuing south, as you round the southern point of Orcas Island, you'll enter the swifter currents of Obstruction Pass, which flow west on the ebb tide. Just to the east of the point is Obstruction Pass Recreation Area, with a fairly protected pebbly beach where you can stop for a break. The area also has nine campsites, also accessible by land from a 0.5-mile trail (via Obstruction Pass) and part of the Cascadia Marine Trail. Currents here and in Peavine Pass to the south of Obstruction Island are challenging and can run up to three to seven knots, though they average considerably less. Tide rips often form off the east end of Obstruction Island. The 215-acre island itself is entirely private, its rocky shores and small beaches off-limits to public access.

As you paddle east of Obstruction Pass and north along the east shore of Orcas Island, you'll reach tiny six-acre Doe Island, which lies about 2.5 miles from Obstruction Pass. Tidelands along two beaches on the way, one just north of Deer Point and the other north of Buoy Bay, are public. Doe Island has five

Kayaking near Obstruction Pass, Orcas Island

campsites, a small trail around the island, and gentle beaches on the south side of the island. From here it's just a short paddle north to Doe Bay Resort, where kayakers and boaters can land in the small cove just to the north of the resort's main building. Nonguests can also leave cars at Doe Bay for a fee of $5.00 per day.

Another worthwhile side trip in the area is out to Peapod Rocks, a cluster of small islets and grassy islands, some of which are covered during high tide, that are part of the national wildlife refuge system in the San Juans. Peapod Rocks are a popular haul-out area for seals and sea lions, and you'll often spot their curious heads bobbing in the water around the refuge if you pay this area a visit. Be sure to stay at least 100 yards from the rocks, however, to avoid disturbing hauled-out seals, particularly the younger pups.

For More Information

Spring Bay Inn (360–376–5531, www.springbayinn.com), located directly adjacent to Obstruction Pass, offers short daily paddles around the Obstruction Pass area for its guests and for other visitors wanting to join.

Doe Island State Marine Park, (360) 378–2044, www.parks.wa.gov/moorage/parks/m_005.asp

3 Point Lawrence–Clark Island

WHAT TO EXPECT: A paddle along the southeast side of Orcas Island and an exposed and challenging crossing of Rosario Strait to a small state marine park

LENGTH: 7 miles out and back from Doe Bay to Clark Island

DIFFICULTY: Most difficult due to exposed open-water crossing, strong eddies, and currents

GETTING THERE: From the Orcas ferry landing, turn left after exiting the ferry and drive Orcas Road (Horseshoe Highway) 7 miles, bearing right at a signed junction toward Moran State Park and the village of East Sound. Continue straight ahead past Crescent Beach, then turn right onto Olga Road. Drive through Moran State Park and turn left onto Point Lawrence Road at the village of Olga, approximately 3 miles from the entrance to Moran State Park. Drive 3 more miles to Doe Bay Resort. Paddlers can launch for free at the resort, and parking is available for a fee of $5.00 a day.

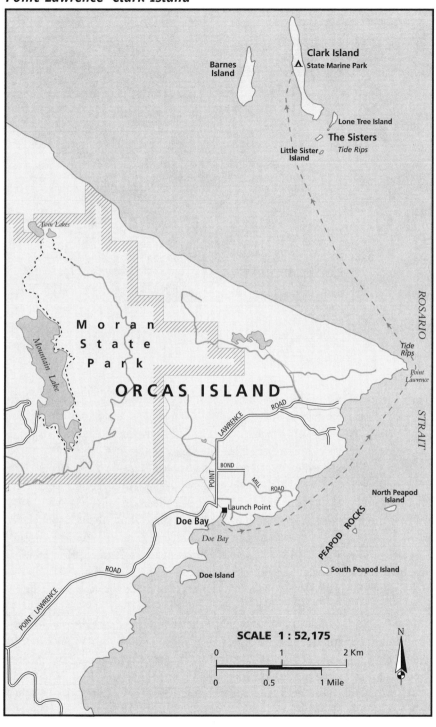

Barnes
Island

Clark Island
State Marine Park

Lone Tree Island

The Sisters

Little Sister
Island

Tide Rips

Twin Lakes

M o r a n
S t a t e
P a r k

Mountain Lake

ORCAS ISLAND

LAWRENCE

ROAD

BOND

POINT

MILL

ROAD

Launch Point

Doe Bay

Doe Bay

ROAD

POINT LAWRENCE

Doe Island

ROSARIO

*Tide
Rips*

*Point
Lawrence*

STRAIT

North Peapod
Island

PEAPOD ROCKS

South Peapod Island

SCALE 1 : 52,175

0   1   2 Km

0   0.5   1 Mile

N

Camping on Clark Island

The Trip

Clark Island, off the eastern tip of Orcas Island, is one of the least visited state marine parks in the San Juans. And while its appeal is that it's off the beaten path, an exposed crossing, strong currents, and notorious tide rips off Point Lawrence make it a trip best suited for advanced paddlers.

Most paddlers heading to Clark Island for the day or an overnight trip launch at Doe Bay on Orcas Island, approximately 3.5 nautical miles from Clark Island. From here, you'll travel northeast along the shore of Orcas, where you can pass the Peapod Rocks National Wildlife Refuge along the way. Tidelands along beaches south of Sea Acres are publicly accessible. Point Lawrence Recreation Site, managed by the state Department of Natural Resources, is largely undeveloped and does not offer any real camping opportunities, but two small pebble beaches on the south side of the point make for a good rest spot if needed.

Once around Point Lawrence, you'll have to navigate an open-water crossing of approximately 2 nautical miles to reach Clark Island. From here the steep, rugged northeast side of Orcas Island comes into view—there's little opportunity to haul out a kayak along this side of the island. Eddies and boils off Point Lawrence can be intense, so it's a good idea to time your trip to round Point Lawrence on a slack tide. The ebb tide flows south here.

At the end of your open-water crossing, you'll first encounter the Sisters to the south of Clark Island, a series of rocks that are part of the San Juan Islands National Wildlife Refuge. Hundreds of pelagic birds come to nest here, including cormorants, pigeon guillemots, and glaucous-winged gulls. To your west is privately owned Barnes Island.

Clark Island's fifty-five acres contain about 2 miles of shoreline, with two upland forested campsites in the middle of the island, along with picnic tables and fire pits, although you'll have to bring your own water. The island also has nine offshore mooring buoys for boaters.

For More Information

Clark Island State Marine Park, (360) 378–2044, www.parks.wa.gov/moorage/parks/m_003.asp

Harbor Seals

As you paddle along the shorelines of the San Juans, don't be surprised to find a few curious harbor seals poking their faces above water for a look at you. With a Puget Sound population of more than 15,000, harbor seals are the most abundant marine mammals around the islands. Although inquisitive, they are generally shy animals that prefer quiet, unpopulated areas.

Adult harbor seals are tan to blue-gray, measuring between 4 and 7 feet long and weighing up to 300 pounds. To distinguish them from other pinnipeds, look for their small size, earless head, and mottled body. And while they may seem less than graceful on land, harbor seals are adept and powerful swimmers, with the ability to swim up to fifteen knots, plunge 300 feet deep, and remain underwater for nearly thirty minutes.

Around the San Juans you'll often see harbor seals "hauled out" on beaches, spits, rocks, or even log rafts to rest, digest food, give birth, or nurse young. Pupping occurs in June and July, and later in the summer season, young pups start to appear hauled out on beaches. Harbor seals can be easily frightened by an approaching boat or kayak, particularly during and after pupping occurs. Scaring pups into the water not only disturbs them, it also requires them to expend precious energy they need for hunting and growth. Do your best to stay at least 100 yards away from hauled-out seals, and to quietly back away from them at the first sign of agitation.

4 Sucia, Matia, and Patos Islands

WHAT TO EXPECT: A challenging open-water crossing to a popular series of islands, with intriguing geology, and numerous camping, hiking, and biking opportunities

LENGTH: 5 miles out and back from Orcas Island to Sucia Island

DIFFICULTY: Most difficult, with strong currents, tide rips, and open-water crossings

GETTING THERE: Most kayakers heading for Sucia Island launch from North Beach on the north side of Orcas Island. From the Orcas ferry landing, turn left onto Orcas Road (Horseshoe Highway) and drive 7 miles to the signed junction for the village of East Sound. Continue straight ahead (north) on Lovers Lane, which bypasses East Sound. Turn right onto Mount Baker Road, passing the airport on your left. At the intersection about 0.2 mile past the airport, turn left onto North Beach Road and drive to the road's end. Parking is limited to a few vehicles. As an alternative, paddlers can park and launch for a fee of $6.00 at Bartwood Lodge to the east of North Beach. Overnight parking is also available here for an additional $6.00 per night.

The Trip

Given how close it lies to the north shore of Orcas Island, it may seem tempting to jump in a kayak and attempt the seemingly short crossing to Sucia Island. It's true that under ideal conditions the 2.5-mile paddle can be made in under an hour, but such conditions are so rare that even professional guiding companies on Orcas Island rarely opt for this trip. Currents along this route are notoriously strong, and challenging rips often form around Parker Reef, particularly on the west-flowing ebb current, making this a trip only for the advanced paddler. For those less skilled at paddling, charters from Orcas will navigate the tricky crossing for you and drop you off at Sucia, along with your paddling and camping gear.

If you do manage to make it to Sucia, lucky you. At over 550 acres, Sucia is actually a complex of eleven main islands, forming the largest state marine park in the San Juans. Sucia offers coves to discover, trails to wander, miles of waterfront to explore, and bizarre geologic formations to ponder. Throw in a bit of history and it's easy to spend a day exploring Sucia by land and another day paddling its many coves.

Geologically, Sucia, Matia, and Patos Islands are relatives, all sharing their characteristic tilted beds of shale and sandstone. The formations are, however, arguably best expressed on Sucia, where you'll find spectacular cliffs, caves, and

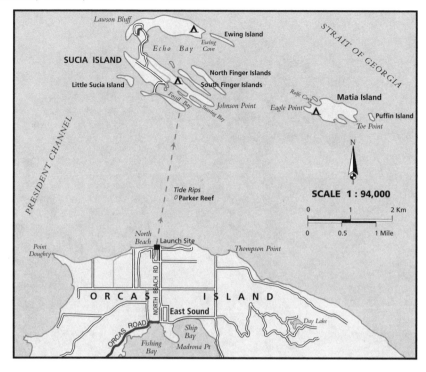

formations sculpted by water and wind, including the bizarre "mushroom" formation in Fox Cove. The island's also home to huge boulders tumbled onto its beaches, including the Chinaman Rock on the northeast side of Shallow Bay, where Chinese being smuggled from Canada into the United States supposedly hid among the rocks.

Several bays and coves on Sucia offer good camping for paddlers—most opt for the more protected east-facing bays. A word of caution though: Sucia is an extremely popular boating destination, and if you come here on a summer weekend or holiday, prepare for lots of company. Echo Bay, the main bay formed by the island's east-facing crescent, and smaller Fossil Bay are popular moorage spots for larger boats. For more solitude, many kayakers head for Ewing Cove at the northeast end of Echo Bay, where three campsites offer a quieter alternative, or to tiny Snoring Bay, between Fossil and Echo Bays. With more than fifty campsites, Sucia is also a popular camping destination, with campsites available largely on a first-come, first-served basis. Reservations are limited to the island's two group campsites—they can be made by contacting Washington State Parks. Drinking water is available on the island from April through November.

Famous mushroom formation, Fox Cove, Sucia Island

On foot, Sucia's 11 miles of trail and road are perfect for exploration. Charter companies will even transport mountain bikes here for you if you're looking for another option for exploring its trails. A service road loops around forested portions of the island, while trails radiate from it to the island's various fingers. From Echo Bay, you can hike out to Lawson Bluff, or head to Ewing Cove, following the trail above Echo Bay that some consider one of the most scenic walks in the San Juans.

Patos Island, 2.5 nautical miles northwest of Sucia, offers equally rewarding exploration for paddlers, with far more solitude. Similar to Sucia, however, kayakers should be aware of potentially rough conditions around the island. Heavy rips form off the east side of the island around Toe Point, and along its north side. The west side of the island is particularly exposed to winds and rough seas, and strong tide rips can form off Alden Point on the west end of the island, where currents from the Strait of Georgia and Boundary Pass converge. The island's seven campsites with restrooms and picnic tables (no potable water) are located at the head of Active Cove on the west side of Patos, where you'll find a pebble beach for launching and landing. Hikers will find a scenic 1.5-mile loop around the island, wandering through forest past the now-abandoned Coast Guard building and 1908 lighthouse on Alden Point, and on to beaches on the north side of the island. The island is administered by the federal Bureau of Land Management with cooperation from Washington State Parks.

Lying 2.5 miles to the east of Sucia is Matia Island, a national wildlife refuge supporting a large colony of puffins, along with other seabirds. Camping is limited to six sites in Rolfe Cove, on the west end of the island, and a 1-mile loop trail that runs down the center of the island, returning along the south shore. Please respect the NO PUBLIC ACCESS signs posted on parts of the island, intended to protect its wildlife. The north side of the island is a particularly popular haul-out spot for seals, and kayakers should keep well away from any hauled-out seals.

Minimizing Your Impact on Wildlife

The increasing volume of boat traffic in the San Juans has caused concerns among scientists due to its impact on local marine mammal and bird populations. Many critics point to the noise and intrusion caused by larger boats, but kayakers can have an impact too. In some cases, because kayakers can approach closer to rocks and shorelines than larger boats, they may have an even greater impact on local wildlife.

If you're a kayaker or other boater, keep a close eye out for nesting birds or seals hauled out on rocks, and avoid approaching closer than 100 yards. For seals, be prepared to slow down and to quickly back away at any signs of agitation. Many marine birds nest around the San Juan Islands from February through October, and approaching too close may flush adult birds from their nests, leaving chicks vulnerable to predation, crushing, or trampling.

Many visitors to the San Juan Islands coming to see the orca whales opt for a trip aboard one of the many commercial whale-watching boats operating throughout the islands (see the sidebar Whale Watching later in this chapter). If you come to watch whales under your own power, familiarize yourself with the whale-watching guidelines published by the National Oceanic and Atmospheric Administration (NOAA). If you encounter whales in a powerboat or sailboat, reduce your speed to less than seven knots within 400 yards of the nearest whale. For all boats, avoid approaching closer than 100 yards to any whale, and if you are within 100 yards, stop and allow the whales to pass. Keep clear of the path of whales by at least 400 yards, and try to limit your whale watching to a maximum of thirty minutes.

The nonprofit group Soundwatch publishes a boater-guidelines pamphlet for viewing wildlife. You can download it from www.whalemuseum.org, or contact the whale museum in Friday Harbor at (800) 946-7227.

Active Cove, Patos Island

For More Information

Osprey Tours (800–529–2567, www.ospreytours.com) runs occasional overnight trips out to Sucia and Patos Islands.

North Shore Charters (360–376–4855, www.sanjuancruises.net) offers charter service from the north shore of Orcas Island, Deer Harbor, and Rosario to outer islands including Sucia, Patos, and Matia Islands. Boats can accommodate bikes and kayaks and can carry passengers right to beach camps.

Bigwave Sea Adventures (800–732–4095, www.bigwaveonline.com) offers a unique 50-mile day circumnavigation of Orcas Island in a high-speed Zodiac, passing Clark, Matia, and Sucia Islands, with a stop at Patos Island.

Sucia, Patos, and Matia Island State Marine Parks, (360) 378–2044, www.parks.wa.gov/moorage/parks (online reservations for Sucia Island)

Matia Island National Wildlife Refuge, (360) 457–8451, http://pacific.fws .gov/refuges/field/wa_sanjuanis.htm

Bureau of Land Management (Patos Island), (509) 665–2100, www.or.blm .gov/spokane

San Juan Island

Being the most diverse, populous, and well known island in the San Juans, San Juan Island has a range of kayaking options for novice and advanced sea kayakers alike. Here you'll find the largest number of guide companies, many of which operate trips along the west side of the island in the hopes of spotting whales. But you'll also find many other opportunities, from the more protected waters of Griffin Bay to longer paddles out to spectacular Stuart Island.

Boaters coming to San Juan or outlying islands will find extensive moorage at Friday Harbor and Roche Harbor, Mitchell Bay, Turn Island (three buoys), Griffin Bay campground (one buoy), and Reid and Prevost Harbors on Turn Island. Larger boats can be launched at Roche Harbor, Friday Harbor, Mitchell Bay, and San Juan County Park.

Kayakers can launch from several points around the island, and those walking on the ferry with their boats can launch at Friday Harbor (launch fee of $5.00 per boat). Other launch sites include Turn Point, Rueben Tarte County Park, San Juan County Park, and Jackson Beach. Launching is also available for a small fee at Roche Harbor and at Snug Harbor Marina and Resort.

5 Griffin Bay

WHAT TO EXPECT: A pleasant day paddle in a protected bay, with a stop at a pebble beach at American Camp

LENGTH: Approximately 10 nautical miles out and back from Jackson Beach

DIFFICULTY: Easy due to weak currents in Griffin Bay and options to avoid open-water crossings

GETTING THERE: From the Friday Harbor ferry landing, turn right then quickly left onto Spring Street. Bear left on Argyle Road and drive approximately 1.25 miles to Pear Point Road. Turn left, then take your first right to reach Jackson Beach and the parking area. Kayaks can be launched from the beach.

The Trip

Griffin Bay, forming a large crescent on the southeast side of San Juan Island, offers a pleasant day's paddling with the potential for a variety of stops along the way, including Griffin Bay State Park and Fourth of July Beach in the American Camp unit of San Juan Island National Historical Park. Currents in the bay

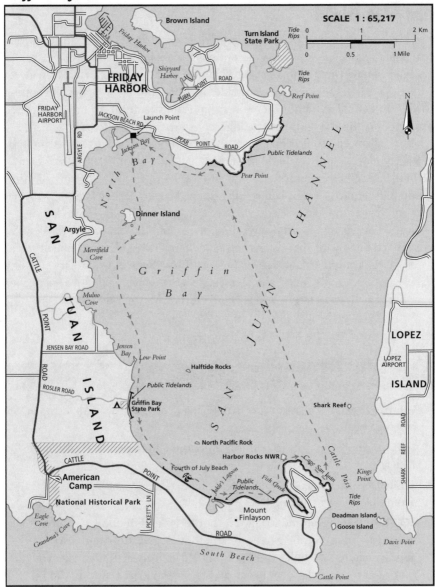

are generally weak, although the bay is exposed to winds that can blow up from the south and east. Jackson Beach, a broad sandy beach at the north end of the bay, makes for a good launching spot for explorations throughout the bay. Kayaks can be rented from a local outfitter right on Jackson Beach.

One of the first stops after launching, just a twenty-minute paddle to the south, is Dinner Island, a small, privately owned island that lacks any public tidelands. You'll often find seals around the rocks just to the south of the island. Another hour of paddling south will bring you past Low Point and on to Fourth of July Beach. If you're planning to camp, Griffin Bay State Park, part of the Cascadia Marine Trail, is located just north of Fourth of July Beach—keep an eye out for the brown STATE PARKS sign along the shoreline.

Fourth of July Beach is a pleasant pebble beach that invites explorations of the meadows behind the beach. Just inland is the old San Juan Town site, the site of the first settlement on the island. American Camp itself also tempts with many worthwhile side trips, including the 3-mile loop hike past Jakle's Lagoon to the summit of Mount Finlayson as described in chapter 2, hike 9.

From here, you can continue to paddle south and west toward the southern tip of San Juan Island, passing the quiet, eelgrass-filled coves of First Lagoon, Jakle's Lagoon, and finally Third Lagoon along the way. Eelgrass beds are ecologically productive nursery areas, providing feeding and cover for juvenile salmon, cod, pollock, herring, and other fishes.

Harbor Rocks National Wildlife Refuge marks the northern tip of Cape San Juan at the southern end of San Juan Island. These rocks are popular haul-out spots for harbor seals. It's best to paddle around the waterward side of the rocks to avoid the dense bull kelp between the rocks and mainland, and to avoid disturbing the seals hauled out here.

Fourth of July Beach, American Camp, San Juan Island

If you're not an experienced kayaker, Harbor Rocks also makes for a good turnaround point. Once around Cape San Juan, you'll enter the distinctly rougher waters of Cattle Pass, not a place for novice kayakers. Currents here are among the strongest in the San Juans, and notoriously large rips develop in the pass between San Juan and Lopez Islands, particularly when winds oppose the current. More skilled kayakers knowledgeable about currents may choose to cross over to the west side of Lopez Island here by timing their crossing with the slack tide and riding the flood tide north along Lopez Island. Don't attempt this crossing, however, unless you're confident in your paddling abilities and skilled in open-water self-rescue.

From here, you can simply retrace your route along the shoreline north back to Jackson Beach or, under calm conditions, make a direct paddle across the open waters of Griffin Bay to Pear Point, then paddle west back to Jackson Beach. Skilled paddlers with more stamina may even explore farther north to Turn Island, but currents and tide rips can be strong here as well.

For More Information

Leisure Kayaks (800–836–1402, www.leisurekayak.com) rents single and double kayaks from their launching site on Jackson Beach.

Griffin Bay State Park, (360) 378–2044

San Juan Island National Historical Park, (360) 378–2902, www.nps.gov/sajh

Turn Island

Just a stone's throw from the shoreline of San Juan Island, Turn Island State Marine Park (360–378–2044, www.parks.wa.gov/moorage/parks/m_017.asp) is more of a destination or stop along a longer paddle trip, rather than a separate paddle trip itself. This pretty little island is a popular spot for camping, and trails around the outside of the island offer views across to Lopez and Shaw Islands, and farther off to Mount Baker. The campsites have picnic tables, toilets, and fire grills, along with their share of aggressive raccoons in the evenings.

6 West Side of San Juan Island

WHAT TO EXPECT: A moderate paddle along the rocky, rugged west side of San Juan Island past a historic lighthouse, with the chance to spot orca whales and other wildlife

LENGTH: 5 miles out and back to Deadman Bay

DIFFICULTY: Moderate; no open-water crossings, but strong currents and potential exposure to rough seas

GETTING THERE: From the ferry landing at Friday Harbor, turn right after exiting the ferry and quickly left onto Spring Street. Turn right onto Blair Avenue and left onto Park Street, which turns into Guard Street, and then Beaverton Valley Road. Follow this road for about 7 miles and turn left onto Mitchell Bay Road, following it for approximately 1.5 miles to West Side Road. Turn left onto West Side Road, where you'll find San Juan County Park in approximately 2 miles on the right. Parking is available next to the administration building, and kayaks can be launched from the adjacent beach.

The Trip

The west side of San Juan Island has become a popular destination for kayakers, particularly guided kayak trips, and for good reason: It's prime whale-watching territory. Each year, from spring to fall, pods of orcas make their way here to feed on salmon migrating through Haro Strait, drawing with them an army of onlookers, from both shore and boat. There's hardly a more exciting prospect than observing one of these majestic animals from the intimacy of a sea kayak. Paddlers here should note, however, that both currents and winds can be strong along this stretch of shoreline due to its exposure to Haro Strait. Novice paddlers should stick close to shore under rough conditions. There are also several guided trips to choose from along this route.

Smallpox Bay in San Juan County Park makes for an excellent launch site, with parking and a gently sloping beach in a protected cove. From here, most paddlers head south, timing their trip with the south-flowing ebb current. If you're paddling against the current, you can stay close to shore to take advantage of back eddies as you head south.

As you round Bellevue Point, you'll soon pass the lime-streaked cliffs and former lime-kiln operations in and around Lime Kiln Point State Park. Limestone operations were important here up until the early 1900s, when San Juan Island was a major source for lime, an important ingredient in mortar. As you pass by, imagine the large ships that used to dock here to load up on lime for shipments south to as far away as San Francisco.

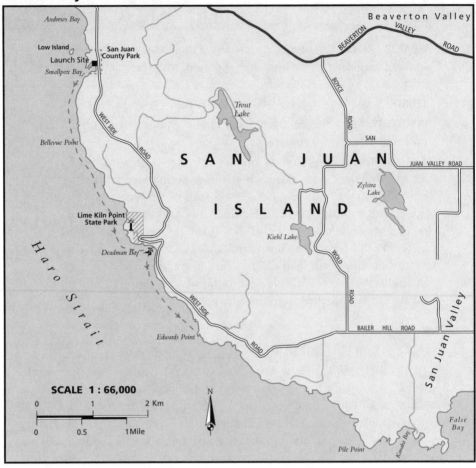

You'll pass the historic lighthouse at Lime Kiln Point (and probably get a friendly wave from onlookers and eager whale watchers on land), soon reaching Deadman Bay. Here you'll find a crescent-shaped pebble beach for a lunch or snack break and the last spot to haul out from this point south until South Beach at American Camp, about another 8.5 miles south. Many guided trips make Deadman Bay or Edwards Point, a mile farther south, their turnaround point for half-day trips.

You can continue south along the shore as far as you'd like, exploring the kelp beds and rocky shoreline, where you may spot hauled-out seals. Also keep an eye out for Dall's porpoises playing in the waters offshore. And when you're ready, simply turn around and retrace your route to San Juan County Park.

For More Information

Outdoor Odysseys (800–647–4621, www.outdoorodysseys.com) runs full-day trips along the west side of San Juan Island.

Sea Quest Expeditions (888–589–4253, www.sea-quest-kayak.com) offers half-day trips along the west side of San Juan Island.

San Juan County Park, (360) 378–8420, www.co.san-juan.wa.us/parks/san juan.html

Paddling past lighthouse at Lime Kiln Point State Park, San Juan Island

Whale Watching

The San Juan Islands have become a mecca for whale watchers, many of whom flock here in summer to catch a glimpse of the orca whale. Most whale watching happens from mid-May to mid-September, although typically the best time to spot orcas is during June and July. You may also see other marine mammals on a whale-watch trip, including minke whales, Dall's porpoises, harbor porpoises, harbor seals, sea lions, and even an occasional elephant seal.

Once a small industry, there are now over eighty operators vying for the attention of whale watchers, most of them located close to the action, on San Juan Island. The Whale Museum in Friday Harbor estimates that more than 500,000 people go whale watching on commercial whale-watch boats in the waters of Washington and British Columbia every year. Not all whale-watching trips are the same—some operators cater more to the crowds with large boats, while others offer a more intimate experience.

With the popularity of whale watching has come concerns about the impact to orca whale populations. While whale watching helps to teach visitors about the biology of orcas, some biologists worry that boats disrupt their feeding and resting behavior, along with their ability to communicate. While researchers continue to investigate, some operators in the San Juan Islands are taking a cautious approach to protect the whales. The Whale Watch Operator's Association Northwest is a group of companies dedicated to responsible wildlife viewing. With the help of marine biologists and researchers, the industry has developed guidelines for operating vessels around the orcas and other wildlife, for both commercial and recreational boaters. Respecting the wildlife and following these guidelines will hopefully help to ensure the safety and health of whale populations for generations to come. The following association members offer trips in the San Juan Islands:

- Bon Accord Charters, (800) 677–0751, www.go-whale-watching.com
- San Juan Excursions, (800) 80–WHALE, www.seewhales.com
- San Juan Safaris, (800) 450–6858, www.sanjuansafaris.com
- Western Prince Cruises, (800) 757–6722, www.orcawhalewatch.com
- Maya's Whale Charters, (360) 378–7996, www.mayaswhalewatch.biz
- Salish Sea Charters, (877) 560–5711, www.salishsea.com
- Orcas Island Eclipse Charters, (800) 376–6566, www.orcasislandwhales.com
- Deer Harbor Charters, (800) 544–5758, www.deerharborcharters.com

WHAT TO EXPECT: An exploration of the islands, passages, and protected bays of the northwest side of San Juan Island

LENGTH: Approximately 6 miles out and back to English Camp

DIFFICULTY: Moderate due to currents in Mosquito Pass

GETTING THERE: From the Friday Harbor ferry landing, turn right off the ferry and quickly left onto Spring Street. Turn right onto Second Street and continue up the hill to a four-way stop. Continue straight to the next three-way stop and turn right onto Tucker Avenue. Continue on this road, which will become Roche Harbor Road. Drive approximately 10 miles and pass through the stone arches for Roche Harbor. Follow signs for the boat launch and parking area. Roche Harbor charges an overnight parking fee of $5.00 per day and a launch fee of $7.00.

The Trip

The many coves and islands around Roche Harbor and Westcott Bay offer a variety of passes, coves, and bays to explore by kayak in a day or afternoon. It's not so much a place with a particular destination but rather a chance to explore

Posey Island State Marine Park

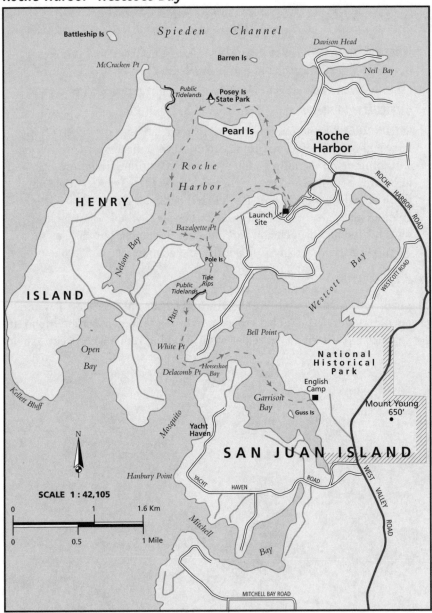

as the currents and your imagination take you through the waters around this corner of San Juan Island. Half-day guided kayak trips also run regularly out of Roche Harbor Marina. The main distraction is that Roche Harbor can be quite busy during the summer boating season, so paddlers will need to remain particularly vigilant to the occasionally heavy boat traffic.

One of the shortest paddles and easiest destinations to reach from Roche Harbor is Posey Island. It's a fairly straightforward twenty-minute paddle out to the one-acre Posey Island State Marine Park, lying just north of Pearl Island, which itself guards the northern entrance to Roche Harbor. On tiny Posey you'll find a campsite (which can only hold one tent), part of the Cascadia Marine Trail. If you're lucky enough to claim the campsite, you'll have a quiet night alone on the island to enjoy the views over Spieden Channel, Haro Strait, and the Gulf Islands beyond to the northwest.

Another option from Roche Harbor is to head south through Mosquito Pass 3 nautical miles to English Camp in Westcott Bay. While Westcott Bay is a protected waterway with minimal current, currents can be strong in Mosquito Pass and tide rips may develop, particularly in the vicinity of Pole Island where currents are funneled over a shallow shelf. The south end of Mosquito Pass is also quite exposed when south winds blow over the open waters of Haro Strait.

Along the way south from Posey Island, take time to explore Nelson Bay on the north side of Henry Island. At the head of the bay, you'll find a series of canals interspersed with dunes, coastal beach, salt marsh, and mudflats. The San Juan Preservation Trust, one of the most active land-preservation groups in the San Juans, has purchased forty-two acres on the isthmus between Nelson and Open Bays to protect the area and may offer public access in the future.

Shallow Westcott Bay itself is a quiet waterway largely free of current, where you can explore Garrison Bay and tiny Guss Island in the south end, and paddle past the shore of English Camp, part of San Juan Island National Historical Park. If you're so inclined, you can stop here and explore the 2-mile trail around Bell Point, or the short interpretive loop around the historic parade grounds of the English Camp (see chapter 2, hike 12). (Note that while you can stop for a break, launching or retrieving kayaks here is prohibited.) When you're ready, just retrace your route back to Roche Harbor.

For More Information

San Juan Safaris (800–450–6858, www.sanjuansafaris.com) runs half-day trips out of Roche Harbor.

Roche Harbor Marina, (800) 451–8910, www.rocheharbor.com/boating_the marina.html

WHAT TO EXPECT: An exposed paddle across a channel with strong currents to waterfront camps and scenic hikes on an island where the San Juans' alternative, rural lifestyle still thrives

LENGTH: 10 miles out and back from Roche Harbor

DIFFICULTY: Most difficult; open-water crossing, strong currents and tide rips in Spieden Channel

GETTING THERE: From the Friday Harbor ferry landing, turn right off the ferry and quickly left onto Spring Street. Turn right onto Second Street and continue up the hill to a four-way stop. Continue straight to the next three-way stop and turn right onto Tucker Avenue. Continue on this road, which will become Roche Harbor Road. Drive approximately 10 miles and pass through the stone arches for Roche Harbor. Follow signs for the boat launch and parking area. Roche Harbor charges an overnight parking fee of $5.00 per day and a launch fee of $7.00.

The Trip

The trip from San Juan Island to Stuart Island is one of the classic overnight paddle trips in the San Juans, crossing the lively and challenging currents of Spieden Channel to the quiet harbors of Stuart Island. While it's possible to do the trip in a day, you'll miss out on the wonders of exploring peaceful Stuart Island, a place that feels like it's just a few notches back in time. There's also the unforgettable experience of catching the sunset from high above the water at Turn Point on the island's western end.

This trip, however, is for advanced paddlers. Spieden Channel is not only an open-water crossing, it's notorious in the islands for its strong currents and tide rips. Add to the mix heavy boat traffic in the summer and you've got a recipe for trouble if you're an inexperienced paddler. Overnight guided trips are available from a few companies operating on San Juan Island.

Many trips to Stuart Island start from Roche Harbor, on San Juan Island's northwest corner. Kayaks can be launched from the Roche Harbor Resort's boat launch, and ample overnight parking is available.

You'll begin your trip by paddling out of the protected waters of Roche Harbor past the impressive (or perhaps excessive) showcase of yachts frequenting the marina, and paddle around Pearl Island. Just north of Pearl Island lies tiny forested Posey Island, a stop on the Cascadia Marine Trail. Just north of Posey lies Barren Island, befitting its name with its lack of trees.

From here, you'll enter the open waters of Spieden Channel for the 2-mile crossing to Spieden Island. Crossings of this channel can be tricky. Tide rips in the channel, particularly around Sentinel Island, can be quite strong, particu-

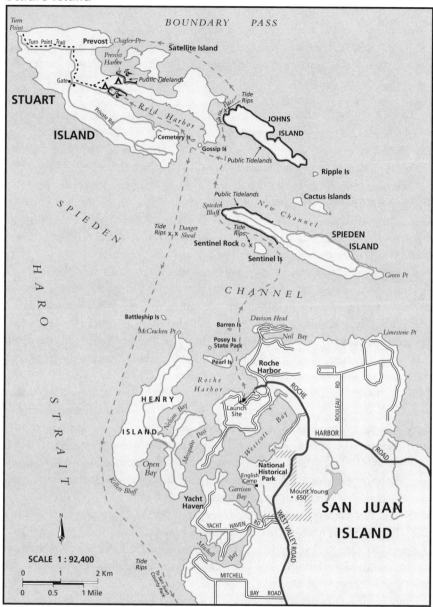

larly on flood tides, and heavy boat traffic in summer can exacerbate the already treacherous conditions. If you're traveling in a group, it's a good place to stay close together to make yourselves more visible to boat traffic. Keep an eye out for minke whales, which have been observed foraging here, or for sea lions, a much larger cousin of the more common harbor seals seen throughout the islands.

Sentinel Island, lying just south of Spieden Island, is owned by the Nature Conservancy and preserved for its outstanding bald-eagle habitat. It was also once the home of June and Farrar Burn, who spent one hundred days sailing around the islands, writing tales of their encounters with island people and places for readers of Seattle newspapers, also publishing a book of their adventures (*100 Days in the San Juans*).

The open, grassy slopes of the south side of 480-acre Spieden Island are the subject of legend in the San Juans. In the 1970s the owner of the island, with grand plans of turning it into a trophy game–hunting farm, introduced a host of exotic ungulates from around the world, including deer from Japan and Europe, antelope from India, sheep, and even wild goats. It seems, however, that later owners weren't so keen on the idea and attempted to hunt down or chase much of the game off the island. In desperation, some of the animals apparently took the plunge, swimming to Stuart Island for refuge. Spieden Island is still privately owned today, and access is not permitted.

As you round the western tip of Spieden Bluff on the west side of the island, look north along its forested shores—you'll notice the dramatic change in vegetation between the north and south sides of the island. The more sheltered north side is lush with Douglas fir, western red cedar, and other conifers, while the south half is largely open grassland. Off in the distance farther north, you'll see the Cactus Islands, part of the national wildlife refuge system in the islands and home to a population of prickly pear cactus.

From here, it's about a 1-mile paddle northwest to the mouth of Stuart Island's Reid Harbor. Stuart Island actually offers two take-out spots for paddlers, one at the head of Reid Harbor and another at Prevost Harbor, on the north side of the island. Reaching Prevost Harbor requires paddling north through Johns Pass, which can experience strong currents and tide rips. From here, it's another 2 miles of paddling past Satellite Island and to Prevost Harbor. You'll find nineteen campsites along the harbor.

The closer option is to paddle into protected Reid Harbor, which also has several forested campsites at the head of the harbor. Along the way you'll pass Gossip Island and Cemetery Island, the latter of which supports a population of several-hundred-year-old Garry oaks, twisted and stunted by exposure to the wind and weather.

Another mile of paddling will bring you to the beach at the head of the harbor. You'll find fourteen good camps here on both sides of the beach, with running water and picnic tables. Those on the north side of the beach are part of the Cascadia Marine Trail system, open only to nonmotorized craft. Nightly moorage fees are $7.00 per night ($16.00 for larger boats). From the camp, you'll find a 0.5-mile trail climbing the bluffs on the north side of the beach, connecting to camps at Prevost Harbor. Camps at both sites can be busy in summer.

Reid Harbor, Stuart Island

Stuart Island itself is a fascinating place, not only for its scenery but also for its community. It's an example of the alternative lifestyle you'll find alive and well in the San Juans, particularly on some of the outer islands. Many of the island's forty or so residents live "off the grid," relying on solar or other energy forms for their power. From camps at the south side of Reid Harbor, you can walk the 2.5 miles of "county road" across the island to Turn Point. The walk, following the colorful hand-painted "street signs" on the way, will give you a good feel for the island's bucolic lifestyle. You'll pass the one-room school-house, where Stuart's dozen or so children go to school (and you can pick up a T-shirt to help support them). From the fields along the road just beyond the school, you can catch the soft evening light on the snowy slopes of Mount Baker. You'll turn left at an intersection and follow this road to Turn Point.

Turn Point, the most northwestern point in the San Juans, sits over 150 feet high on a grassy bluff overlooking Haro Strait, with spectacular views across to Canada's Vancouver Island and Gulf Islands. The federal Bureau of Land Management administers sixty acres at Turn Point, including the island's historic lighthouse-keepers quarters, just to the north of the point. Buildings at Turn Point were first constructed in 1893, and now the Coast Guard–managed horn house is fully automated. Enjoy the sunset here, watching the porpoises play in the currents offshore, and keep an eye out for orca whales, also visiting the waters here in search of salmon.

When you're ready to leave Stuart Island, you'll have a few options for returning to San Juan Island. Many will choose to simply retrace their route to Roche Harbor, but under favorable ebb tides and weather conditions, it's possible to paddle the 11 or so miles to San Juan County Park on the west side of San Juan Island, passing the rugged west side of Henry Island along the way (keep an eye out for the large cormorant colony). Note that this route is significantly more exposed, and that tide rips can develop around Danger Shoal in Spieden Channel. Tide rips can also develop south of Henry Island, where currents from Mosquito Pass collide with currents in Haro Strait. During rough weather in Haro Strait, yet another option is to paddle the more protected route through Mosquito Pass.

For More Information

Outdoor Odysseys (800–647–4621, www.outdoorodysseys.com) offers multiday trips to Stuart Island and along the west shore of San Juan Island.

Sea Quest Expeditions (888–589–4253, www.sea-quest-kayak.com) offers overnight trips to Stuart Island from San Juan Island.

Stuart Island State Marine Park, (360) 378–2044, www.parks.wa.gov/moorage/parks/m_015.asp

Roche Harbor Marina, (800) 451–8910, www.rocheharbor.com/boating_the marina.html

Bureau of Land Management (Turn Point), (509) 665–2100, www.or.blm .gov/spokane

Reuben Tarte Park

Public access to the shoreline has become an increasing concern in the San Juans, and Reuben Tarte Park, on the east side of San Juan Island, offers the only public water access from Friday Harbor north and west to Roche Harbor. It's a popular take-out spot for kayakers and a good place for a break if you're planning a paddle along this side of San Juan Island from Roche Harbor or Friday Harbor. The pocket pebble beach lies in a cove protected by rocky bluffs, offering views east toward Jones Island and the Wasp Islands, and north to Waldron Island. Tiny O'Neil Island lies just offshore to the southeast, while Green Point on the eastern tip of Spieden Island is visible to the north.

Lopez Island

Quiet, serene Lopez Island is a good place to get away from it all, whether you're on the land or water. Positioned at the south end of the San Juan archipelago, it's got the most irregular shoreline of the three main islands, giving paddlers a lot of shoreline to explore, from Lopez Sound to the wild, rugged south shore. If you're coming to Lopez on the ferry, the one limitation is that you won't be able to launch at the ferry landing—the nearest launch site is Odlin County Park, about a mile from the ferry landing. Other launch sites include Mud Bay County Park; Hunter Bay, near the Sperry Peninsula; MacKaye Harbor; Agate Beach; Fisherman Bay; and Spencer Spit State Park. And while choices are more limited than on the other islands, both kayak rentals and guided trips are available on Lopez Island.

Those arriving at Lopez Island by boat will find sixteen mooring buoys at Spencer Spit on the east side of the island from spring through fall and three mooring buoys during summer at Upright Channel Picnic Area. Odlin County Park has a boat launch, float, and dock, and launching is also available at Hunter Bay and MacKaye Harbor. On nearby islands, James Island has a dock, float, and four mooring buoys, while boaters will find four buoys at Blind Island State Marine Park. Moorage and a boat launch can also be found at South Beach Park on the east side of Shaw Island.

9 Shaw Island

WHAT TO EXPECT: A protected day paddle on the east side of Shaw Island, or a longer moderate circumnavigation of the island

LENGTH: Approximately 15-mile circumnavigation

DIFFICULTY: Easy to moderate. Currents are weak in Upright Channel but stronger in Harney and San Juan Channels.

GETTING THERE: From the Lopez Island ferry landing, drive approximately 1 mile on Ferry Road. The signed entrance for Odlin County Park will be on your right. Kayaks can be launched from the sandy beach, and parking is available.

The Trip

Shaw Island is one of the more popular paddling spots in the San Juan Islands. Fairly protected with lots of wild shoreline to explore, Shaw Island offers trips for all levels and of many lengths, from a quiet afternoon exploring Indian Cove and Squaw Bay on the east side of the island, to a longer 15-mile full-day

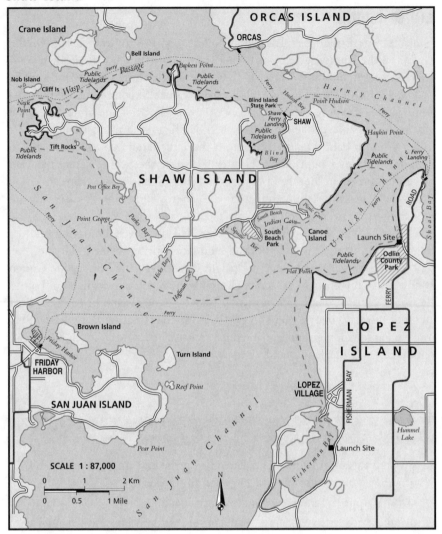

circumnavigation. While easily reached from the launch at Turn Point on San Juan Island, many choose to start their trip from the more protected Odlin County Park or Fisherman Bay on Lopez. Those without kayaks can rent boats and equipment at Fisherman Bay.

From Odlin County Park or Fisherman Bay, the easiest crossing over to Shaw Island is via the 0.25-mile crossing of Upright Channel just off of Flat Point. While it's a short distance, you'll be crossing the ferry route here, so make sure to be aware of oncoming ferry traffic.

Canoe Island protects the entrance to Indian Cove on Shaw Island, where Shaw Island's scenic South Beach, one of the best beaches in the San Juans, offers a tempting take-out spot for a break or lunch stop (overnight camping is also available here). Note that at low tides, mudflats in the shallow cove may make paddling difficult. The fifty-acre Canoe Island is privately owned and home to Canoe Island French Camp, a language-and-culture summer camp for children. All of Canoe's tidelands are public.

North of Indian Cove is tiny Picnic Cove, and north beyond that the forested, undeveloped east side of Shaw Island. Currents here are generally weak, and tidelands here (below mean high water) are publicly owned. For those just looking for a short paddle, a crossing of Upright Channel to Upright Head (again watching for ferry traffic) makes for a quick trip back to Odlin County Park. For those paddling from Fisherman Bay, simply retrace the Lopez shoreline south back to Fisherman Bay.

If you're looking to paddle farther, you can travel west around Hankin Point, the eastern tip of Shaw, entering Harney Channel. From here, it's another 1.6 miles to two-acre Blind Island State Marine Park, just offshore of the Shaw Island ferry landing. Approximately 4.5 miles from Odlin County Park, the island offers another opportunity for a break, or even an overnight stay at one of the island's four campsites, part of the Cascadia Marine Trail. The island, however, is popular and sees heavy boat use. It's hard to imagine, but the tiny island was once home to a small number of residents who extracted oil from dogfish livers to sell for its vitamin content. If you're exploring Shaw Island's Blind Bay, tidelands are public along a section of the western side of the bay.

Blind Island State Marine Park

If you're continuing around the island, from Blind Bay you'll paddle west through Harney Channel, around Broken Point, and through Wasp Passage. From Broken Point west to Neck Point, beware of paddling midchannel, as you'll be on the ferry route from Orcas Island to San Juan Island.

Once around Neck Point, most tidelands on the west side of Shaw Island are in private ownership and currents are stronger here in San Juan Channel. South of Neck Point you'll pass the grassy Tift Rocks National Wildlife Refuge. At the south end of the island, you'll pass Hoffman Cove, with scenic shoreline and pebble beaches that are part of the University of Washington's biological preserve on the island. (Access here is discouraged to protect the natural values of the preserve.)

From here, it's a short paddle to the south side of Canoe Island and across to Flat Point on Lopez Island. Simply retrace your route from here back to either Odlin County Park or Fisherman Bay.

For More Information

Lopez Kayaks (360–468–2847, www.lopezkayaks.com) rents kayaks from its waterside location at Fisherman Bay.

Odlin County Park, (360) 378–8420, www.co.san-juan.wa.us/parks/lopez .html

10 Lopez Sound–James Island

WHAT TO EXPECT: A paddle past several islands in Lopez Sound through the exposed Rosario Strait to a scenic state marine park

LENGTH: Approximately 12 miles out and back

DIFFICULTY: Moderate to most difficult. Strong currents around Decatur Head, exposure to strong winds on Rosario Strait.

GETTING THERE: From the Lopez Island ferry landing, drive Ferry Road south for 2.1 miles and turn left onto Center Road. Drive 5.8 miles on Center Road, which turns into Mud Bay Road. Drive an additional 2.2 miles and turn left onto Islandale Road. Drive 1.4 miles to the road's end and the Hunter Bay dock. Parking is available, and kayaks can be launched from the boat ramp area.

The Trip

James Island, located just east of Decatur Island, is a popular state marine park and a worthy destination for a paddle trip. It's also part of the Cascadia Marine

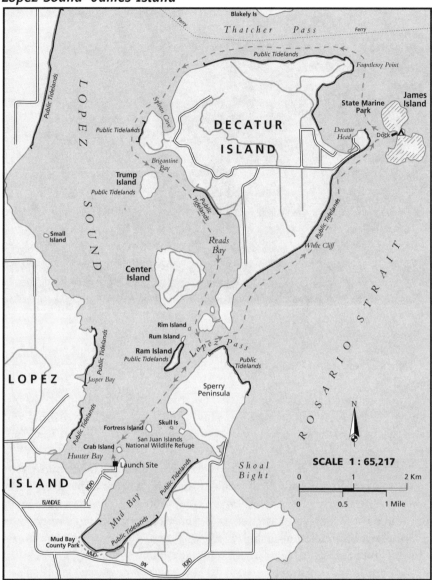

Trail. Lopez Island makes for a good jumping-off point for the island, either from Spencer Spit to the north or from the Hunter Bay dock on the south side of the island. The trip from Hunter Bay is probably the more interesting of the two routes, passing several small islands that are part of the national wildlife refuge system, and avoiding ferry and boat traffic in Thatcher Pass. Advanced paddlers also occasionally make the open and exposed crossing of Rosario Strait

Harbor seal

to James Island from Anacortes when currents and weather conditions are favorable.

From Hunter Bay you'll pass Crab, Fortress, and Skull Islands, all part of the national wildlife refuge system. While Lopez Bay is protected from currents, winds from the south can funnel across the south end of Lopez Island and create rough conditions here.

Continuing north, you'll pass Ram Island, privately owned with public tidelands, and tiny Rum Island, then turn east through narrow Lopez Pass. From here you're entering the more exposed waters of Rosario Strait—under rough conditions it's advisable to stay close to the shore of Decatur Island, where most tidelands are in public ownership. It's best to time your trip with the north-flowing flood current, which can be strong around both sides of James Island.

Decatur Island is privately owned and home to fewer than one hundred permanent residents. Miles of scenic roads are open to the public, but there is no public land to speak of. Public tidelands at White Cliff Beach on the southeast side of the island, however, do offer rest opportunities. Center Island, at just under 200 acres, is private.

James Island, about 2 miles from Lopez Pass, has thirteen campsites with picnic tables and more than a mile of hiking trails, but you'll have to bring your own drinking water. The Cascadia Marine Trail site can be found on the southwest side of the island.

From here, you can simply retrace your route back to Hunter Bay, or as an alternative continue north around Fuantleroy Point, west through Thatcher Pass, and south along Decatur Island back to Hunter Bay, which will add approximately 2.5 miles to the return trip.

For More Information

James Island State Marine Park, (360) 378–2044, www.parks.wa.gov/moorage/parks/m_007.asp

11 Lopez Island's South Shore

WHAT TO EXPECT: Rocky shorelines, numerous bays, and abundant wildlife on the wild south shore of Lopez Island

LENGTH: 7 miles out and back to Iceberg Point

DIFFICULTY: Moderate due to exposure to wind and waves

GETTING THERE: From the Lopez Island ferry landing, drive south on Ferry Road for 2.1 miles and turn left onto Center Road. After 5.8 miles, Center Road turns into Mud Bay Road. Drive Mud Bay Road 3 miles and turn right onto MacKaye Harbor Road. Turn quickly right and follow this road to its end at the MacKaye Harbor boat ramp. Parking is available on the small hill just above the ramp.

The Trip

The south shore of Lopez is a paradise for paddlers, with quiet harbors, dramatic cliffs, abundant wildlife, the chance to spot whales in season, and islands and rocks to explore—all without the crowds you'll find in many other kayaking spots. While launching areas are limited, you'll have plenty of options for exploring once you're in the water. Guided trips are available in the area as well.

MacKaye Harbor makes for the best launch spot on the south side of the island, where you'll find a concrete boat ramp and parking. If you choose to launch at Agate Beach, you'll have to carry your kayak down a set of stairs to the beach. Off-street parking is also limited to only a few cars here.

MacKaye Harbor itself is quiet and protected from currents, and you can silently glide past forested shorelines, admire hilltop homes, and watch the orange-eyed black oystercatchers perch along the rocky shoreline. Heading west out of MacKaye Harbor, it's about 1.6 miles to the former Richardson store site and fuel dock, dating back to the late 1800s when the south side of Lopez was a bustling port for the salmon-fishing industry.

Lopez Island's South Shore

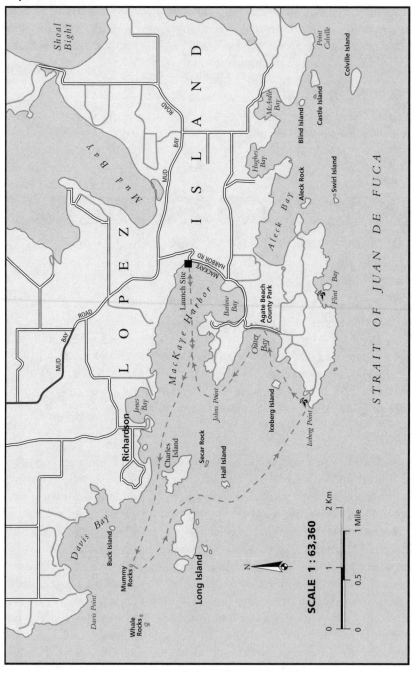

SCALE 1 : 63,360

N

Shoal
Bight

Mud Bay

L O P E Z   I S L A N D

MUD BAY ROAD

ROAD

MUD BAY ROAD

Richardson

Jones
Bay

Charles
Island

Secar Rock

Hall Island

Johns Point

MacKaye Harbor

Launch Site

MACKAYE HARBOR RD

Barlow
Bay

Otter
Bay

Agate Beach
County Park

Iceberg Island

Iceberg Point

Aleck Bay

Aleck Rock

Hughes
Bay

McArdle
Bay

Blind Island

Swirl Island

Castle Island

Colville Island

Point
Colville

Flint
Bay

S T R A I T   O F   J U A N   D E   F U C A

Davis Bay

Davis Point

Buck Island

Mummy
Rocks

Whale
Rocks

Long Island

0   1   2 Km

0   0.5   1 Mile

From here, you can work your way farther west past privately owned Charles Island to Mummy Rocks National Wildlife Refuge, a scattering of small rocks that provide haul-outs for seals and nesting for a variety of seabirds. Mummy Rocks make a good westward turnaround point, as beyond lies Cattle Pass, where currents and tide rips are typically strong.

Heading back east, you'll pass Long Island, where you may spot orca whales during summer and early fall as they swim up and down the shore of San Juan Island in search of salmon. You'll also pass Hall Island and Secar Rock National Wildlife Refuges, where double-breasted and pelagic cormorants, black oyster-catchers, pigeon guillemots, and glaucous winged gulls nest, sharing the islands with harbor seals and river otters.

Iceberg Point, managed by the federal Bureau of Land Management, is a ruggedly scenic spot, where bare, rocky cliffs plunge into the sea, and forests of bull kelp sway in the currents offshore. Here, you may see tufted puffins foraging in the vicinity of Iceberg Point. Farther east, Colville Island, off of Point Colville, is the only place where tufted puffins are known to nest in the San Juan Islands. Just north of Iceberg Point is Iceberg Island, a state marine park where day use is allowed.

MacKaye Harbor, Lopez Island

If you're in the mood for a hike, you'll find a small beach at the north end of the small cove just north of Iceberg Point, with a primitive trail scrambling up the bluffs. Here, you can combine a paddle trip with a 2-mile out-and-back hike to Iceberg Point (see chapter 2, hike 16).

If you travel farther east beyond Iceberg Point along the south shore of Lopez, be aware that this side of the island is very exposed to swells and rough seas on south winds. It's also a very rugged stretch of shoreline, where rocky cliffs offer little shelter in poor conditions. If you were to continue paddling east, the next opportunity to land is on public tidelands at McArdle Bay, while the next take-out spot is not until Mud Bay in Lopez Sound. While the beach at Hughes Bay is accessible, the steep flight of stairs to the beach does not make for a good take-out point.

Otherwise, simply retrace the shoreline of Outer Bay, around Johns Point, and back to MacKaye Harbor.

For More Information

Lopez Kayaks (360–468–2847, www.lopezkayaks.com) runs half-day trips along the south shore of Lopez Island.

Island Outfitters (360–299–2300, www.seakayakshop.com), in partnership with a charter service that transports paddlers out to Lopez, runs kayak day trips to the south shore of Lopez from Anacortes.

Bureau of Land Management, Spokane District, (509) 665–1200, www.or.blm.gov/spokane

Other Islands in the San Juans

Blakely Island: Blakely is a large, hilly, and heavily forested island with two lakes, located just south of Obstruction Island. While most of the island is private, visitors arriving by boat are welcome at the public marina on the north tip of the island, where there's even a small general store. Guest moorage is available.

Waldron Island: Waldron Island, located 1.5 miles northwest of Orcas Island across President Channel, is a large, marshy, flat, mostly private, and somewhat mysterious island. While its roads and a dock are open to the public, the general feeling in the San Juans is that Waldron Islanders generally prefer to be left alone. About 480 acres on the island are owned by The Nature Conservancy and the San Juan Preservation Trust. Day use is allowed.

Cypress Island

WHAT TO EXPECT: A circumnavigation of a heavily forested, rugged, undeveloped island, with some challenging rips and currents, and overnight camping opportunities

LENGTH: 15 miles

DIFFICULTY: Moderate to most difficult due to strong tide rips and currents in some locations

GETTING THERE: To launch from the Guemes Island Ferry Terminal, follow Highway 20 Spur (Commercial Avenue) into Anacortes and turn left, following the signed route to the San Juan ferries from downtown Anacortes. In 0.25 mile, turn north onto I Street and drive to the Guemes Island Ferry Terminal. Parking is limited. Washington Park can be found by driving farther west, past the San Juan Islands ferry terminal.

The Trip

Cypress Island, with its miles of wild coastline and lively currents, remains a mystery to many visitors to the San Juans, as it's off the main ferry route and offers little to those who are seeking the comforts of civilization. Yet it's these very qualities that make it a worthwhile and popular paddling destination. Only a small portion of the 8.5-square-mile island was homesteaded in the 1800s, and today over 90 percent of the island is undeveloped wild shoreline. Three camps on and around the island are part of the Cascadia Marine Trail (Cypress Head, Pelican Beach, and Strawberry Island), and an overnight stay will give you the chance to walk through the island's quiet forests and experience its true wildness (you'll have to bring your own water). Due to its popularity with kayakers, several outfitters offer guided trips to and around the island.

The main way of approaching Cypress by kayak starts from Anacortes near the Guemes Island Ferry Terminal, following the west shore of Guemes Island. Other more experienced paddlers may choose the more exposed crossing from Washington Park, farther west. A complete circumnavigation of the island is approximately 15 miles.

From the launch site south of Guemes, you'll paddle across the short Guemes Channel (the ebb flows west here), then north, following the west shore of Guemes Island. Those skilled enough to time their trips right can pad-

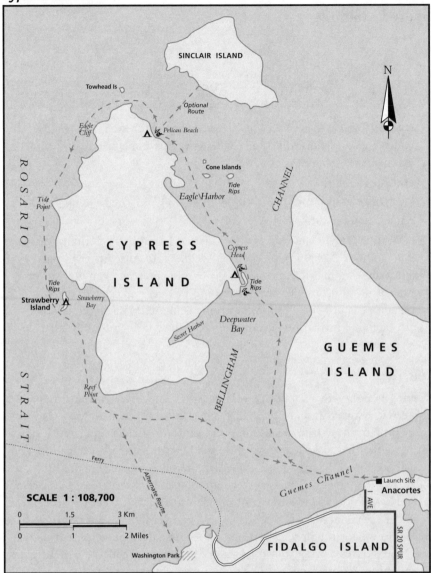

dle with the last of the ebb tide west through Guemes Channel, then ride the flood tide north along the west side of Guemes Island.

After about 3 miles of paddling, you'll spot Cypress Head, a hammer-shaped point of land on the east side of Cypress Island. Here, you'll find a Washington Department of Natural Resources recreation site with several scenic primitive campsites along bluffs looking over the water. Pebble beaches on both the south and north sides of the tombolo that connects Cypress Head to the main island make good landing points.

Cypress Head is notorious for its strong tide rips and currents that form a few hundred feet offshore of the head, particularly on ebb tides. To make this crossing, you can either time your travels through the area during slack tide, or cross south of the head and stay close to shore. If you're camping here, you may even wish to take out at the beach on the south side of the head.

From Cypress Head it's about another 3 miles of paddling north to Pelican Beach, offering another good campsite for paddlers. Currents can be strong around the Cone Islands. For a quick side trip, about a mile to the northeast is Sinclair Island, a small and mostly private island. There is a county dock on the southwest side of the island, where you can take out and walk the island's back roads and check out the thirty-five-acre Sinclair Island National Wildlife Refuge. Pelican Beach also makes a good base for spending a day hiking Cypress Island, including trips to Eagle Cliff (seasonally closed to protect threatened, endangered, and sensitive species), Duck Lake, or Eagle Cove.

If you're continuing around Cypress Island, take caution that the waters on the rugged west side of the island can be rough, being exposed to Rosario Strait, particularly around the west side of Strawberry Island. Three campsites on Strawberry Island are also part of the Cascadia Marine Trail. From here, it's either a 5-mile paddle back to Washington Park, or you can continue around the island, cross Bellingham Channel, and return to the Guemes ferry landing.

For More Information

Island Outfitters (360–299–2300, www.seakayakshop.com) runs kayak day and overnight trips to and around Cypress Island.

Moondance Sea Kayak Adventures (360–738–7664, www.moondance kayak.com) runs trips to Cypress Island.

Cone Islands, off Cypress Island

Elakah! Expeditions (800–434–7270) also runs kayak trips to Cypress Island. Washington Department of Natural Resources, Northwest Region, (360) 856–3500

More Resources

Kayak Companies: Orcas Island

- Shearwater Adventures (360–376–4699, www.shearwaterkayaks.com) offers three-hour and full-day tours, along with moonlight and custom tours to various locations around Orcas Island.
- Orcas Outdoors Sea Kayak Tours (360–376–4611, www.orcasoutdoors.com), located at Orcas Island Ferry Landing, offers daily trips of one to three hours in West Sound and overnight tours.
- Osprey Tours (800–529–2567, www.ospreytours.com) offers tours in hand-crafted kayaks built in the design of Aleutian Eskimos of Alaska.
- Crescent Beach Kayaks (360–376–2464) rents kayaks at its beachside location, just east of the village of East Sound, for paddles on East Sound.
- Spring Bay Inn (360–376–5531, www.springbayinn.com) offers short morning and sunset guided tours for its guests and others in the Obstruction Pass area.

Charters and Other Services: Orcas Island

- North Shore Charters (360–376–4855, www.sanjuancruises.net) offers custom fishing and recreation charters from the north shore, Deer Harbor, and Rosario on Orcas Island, including kayaking, hiking, or mountain-biking trips to Sucia, Matia, and Patos Islands.
- Bigwave Sea Adventures (800–732–4095, www.bigwaveonline.com) provides a 50-mile day trip that circumnavigates Orcas Island in a high-speed Zodiac 733 Hurricane.
- Orcas Boat Rentals/Charters (360–376–7616, www.orcasboats.com) provides chartered cruises to outer islands, sunset cruises, and bareboat rentals of Catalina sailboats, runabouts, and duraboats.
- Northwest Classic Daysails (360–376–5581, www.classicdaysails.com) offers afternoon or evening sails from Deer Harbor.
- Emerald Isle Sailing Charters (866–714–6611, www.emeraldislesailing.com) provides crewed sailing trips through the San Juan and Gulf Islands, the Inside Passage, and the Great Bear Rainforest of northern British Columbia.

Kayak Companies: San Juan Island

- Leisure Kayaks (800–836–1402, www.leisurekayak.com) rents single or double kayaks and offers two-hour tours from its Jackson Beach location.
- Outdoor Odysseys (800–647–4621, www.outdoorodysseys.com) offers guided day trips along the west side of San Juan Island, multiday trips out to Stuart Island, and a multiday bed-and-breakfast tour around the islands. Multiday expeditions through Seattle-based REI. Custom tours are also available.
- Sea Quest Kayak Expeditions (888–589–4253, www.sea-quest-kayak.com) provides guided trips with guides trained as biologists, including day trips on the west side of San Juan Island, along with two- to five-day camping trips.
- San Juan Safaris (800–450–6858, www.sanjuansafaris.com) offers three-hour trips from Roche Harbor, as well as longer day and overnight trips.
- Crystal Seas Kayaking (877–SEAS–877, www.crystalseas.com) runs three-hour and full-day trips on the west side of San Juan Island, as well as multiday camping, inn-to-inn, and multisport (biking and kayaking) trips.
- Discovery Sea Kayak (360–378–2559, www.discoveryseakayak.com) offers day trips on the west side of San Juan Island and multiday trips throughout the islands.
- San Juan Kayak Expeditions (360–378–4436, www.sanjuankayak.com) offers three- and four-day trips throughout the San Juan Islands (including kayak sailing!).

Charters and Other Services: San Juan Island

(See also the "Whale Watching" sidebar earlier in this chapter.)

- San Juan Island Commuter (800–443–4552, www.islandcommuter.com) cruises from Bellingham to fourteen islands around the San Juans.
- Chiron Charters (360–370–5678, www.chironcharters.com) offers two sailing trips a day from Roche Harbor.
- Charters Northwest (800–258–3119, www.chartersnw.com) offers skippered and bareboat chartered yachts and powerboats from Friday Harbor.

Lopez Island Kayak Companies

- Lopez Sea Kayak (360–468–2847, www.lopezkayaks.com) runs day trips along the south side of Lopez Island and sunset kayak trips. Kayaks can also be rented from its Fisherman Bay location.

Lopez Island Charters

- Harmony Charters (360–468–3310, www.interisland.net/countess/home
.htm) provides skippered cruises throughout the San Juan Islands.
- Kismet Charters (360–468–243, www.rockisland.com/~sailkismet/default
.htm) offers full-day and multiday sailing trips throughout the San Juan and
Gulf Islands.

Off-Island Kayak Guides

- Anacortes-based Island Outfitters (866–445–7506, www.seakayakshop.com)
offers rentals and runs trips to Yellow Island and the south shore of Lopez
Island, as well as to Cypress, James, and other islands throughout the San
Juans.
- Moondance Sea Kayak Adventures (360–738–7664, www.moondance
kayak.com) offers half-day, full-day, and multiday trips to Cypress Island, as
well as in the Bellingham and Vancouver Island areas.

Chapter 4:
Exploring the Roads

If you're looking to get a real flavor for life in the San Juans, one of the best ways to do so is to explore their roads and trails by bike. The size of the islands, combined with their low traffic volumes and quiet back roads, makes them a popular destination for cyclists. You can ride gentle country roads past bucolic farmland on Lopez or soak in the sweeping views over Haro Strait on San Juan Island's West Side Road. Those looking to give their legs a good workout will find challenge in the hillier terrain of Orcas Island, and you can even catch an adrenaline-pumping ride on the single-track mountain trails in Orcas Island's Moran State Park.

Summer is peak biking season in the islands—come during this time and you're likely to be sharing the road with fellow cyclists, especially on Lopez and San Juan Islands. Both are popular destinations not only for weekend cyclists, but also for the several tour groups that now offer multiday trips in the islands. Fall and spring can be especially pleasant times for cycling, with cool to mild weather and fewer crowds. In fact, if you're a mountain biker, more than half of Moran State Park's trails, where you'll find the most challenging terrain, are only open to mountain bikers during the off-season.

Stronger road cyclists can complete circuits of both San Juan and Lopez Islands in an afternoon or a day, while Orcas Island's terrain and road layout feature both steeper climbs and more backtracking. Of course, more casual cyclists will find several shorter loop trips on each island, along with pleasant opportunities to stop along the way for food, sightseeing, or just enjoying the scenery. The trips in this book not only describe some suggested cycling

Cycling Safety Tips

While cycling in the San Juans is a relatively safe experience, many roads are narrow and lack shoulders—sometimes you'll find yourself in uncomfortably tight quarters with local traffic. Here are a few tips to make your ride a safer one:

- If you're in a group, ride single file.

- Avoid stopping on curves, hills, or other places not in sight of oncoming motorists.

- Be aware that all traffic laws apply to bikes as well.

- And, of course, always wear a helmet!

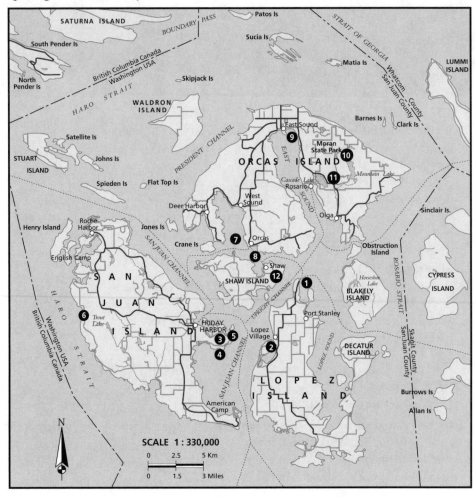

routes on each island, but also share some of the sights worth seeing along the way. Give yourself plenty of time for wandering.

Of course, for those short on time or looking for a less ambitious experience, the routes in this book are just as well suited for touring by car. But whichever way you go, don't be afraid to head off and explore side roads—you just might find some pleasant surprises.

Cycling Tours

With the growing tourism industry in the San Juans, cycling tours have increasingly become a popular way of seeing the islands. During the summer it's now quite common to come across larger groups touring the islands. There's a wide choice of trips available, and some companies are even offering multiday, multisport excursions that combine cycling on all of the larger islands with hikes, kayak trips, and other activities. If you're looking for an organized tour, here are some companies worth a look:

Bicycle Adventures (800–443–6060, www.bicycleadventures.com) offers multiday trips, including camping or family-oriented tours.

Backroads (800–GO–ACTIVE, www.backroads.com), known for its trips all over the world, offers six-day trips in the San Juans, with stays at inns or campgrounds.

TerraTrek (888–441–2433, www.goterratrek.com) offers two- to six-day tours of the islands, with inn stays or camping.

Lopez Island

Pastoral Lopez Island is a cyclist's paradise, a place where you can pedal past rolling farmland, take in spectacular shoreline views, and experience the rich agricultural history of the San Juans. You'll find an abundance of historic buildings on the island dating back to the mid-1800s, a legacy of the generations of families that have lived and farmed the landscape here. With a high point of less than 500 feet, Lopez also offers gentler terrain compared to the other islands, more options for side trips, and relatively less traffic. Many of the back roads remain unstriped (striping roads can be quite a controversy in the San Juans), and it's not uncommon to have the road to yourself.

While strong cyclists can easily finish the 35 miles it takes to do a complete loop around the island in an afternoon, there's plenty of reasons to take time and stop to explore Lopez along the way. Several of the island's short hikes described in chapter 2 can easily be combined with a day of cycling. You can also stop for a meal or to explore cozy Lopez Village, or visit some of the island's local farms, some of which are open to the public in the summer months.

Tour de Lopez

If you find yourself on Lopez Island in spring, you might just catch the non-competitive Tour de Lopez, the island's annual bike tour that follows routes through scenic island landscapes, usually ending with a community outdoor barbecue, followed by music and dancing at local restaurants. Check with the island's chamber of commerce (360–468–4664, www.lopezisland.com) for the latest details.

If you're interested in the island's farming community, a helpful resource is the Lopez Island Farm Products Guide (http://sanjuan.wsu.edu/pdf/Lopez Guide.pdf; call the Lopez Community Land Trust at 360–468–3723 for updates). This handy guide provides a map and descriptions of the island's working farm community to promote and support local agriculture. If you do plan some farm visits, it's usually best to call ahead as schedules may vary seasonally and are subject to change.

1 North End of Lopez Island

WHAT TO EXPECT: Tour the north half of Lopez Island, cycling past Odlin County Park, Spencer Spit State Park, Lopez Island Vineyard, Hummel Lake, Lopez Village, and Otis Perkins Day Park

APPROXIMATE LENGTH: 14 miles

DIFFICULTY: Moderate due to some moderate hill climbs

The Ride

This scenic loop, originating at the Lopez ferry dock, will give you a good introduction to the north half of the island, with its historic farms, beaches, and rural shoreline. Along the way, you'll have the chance to visit three of the island's waterfront parks, where you can explore the shoreline or take one or several short hikes. The shops and restaurants of Lopez Village also make for a worthwhile stop.

While this ride is over mostly gentle terrain, you'll confront the island's most notorious hill in the initial 0.5 mile heading south from the ferry dock. In about a mile you'll come to the entrance to Odlin County Park, where you can take two short walks (see chapter 2, hike 13) or simply stop to explore the sandy beach. Odlin County Park also offers good beachside camping for those touring by bike or car.

From here, the route turns left onto Port Stanley Road, passing by a few homes before coming to scenic Swifts Bay in less than a mile, where the road hugs the beach, with views across to Blakely Island. The shore is predominantly private here, but one small roadside spot along the south side of the bay provides limited public access.

Before the road climbs away from Swifts Bay, you'll pass the Port Stanley Community Hall, a two-story, vertical-sided building constructed in 1889 and originally used as a community meeting place. In its brighter days, islanders conducted church services on the first floor, while parties and dances were held

Lopez Island Cycling (Rides 1 and 2)

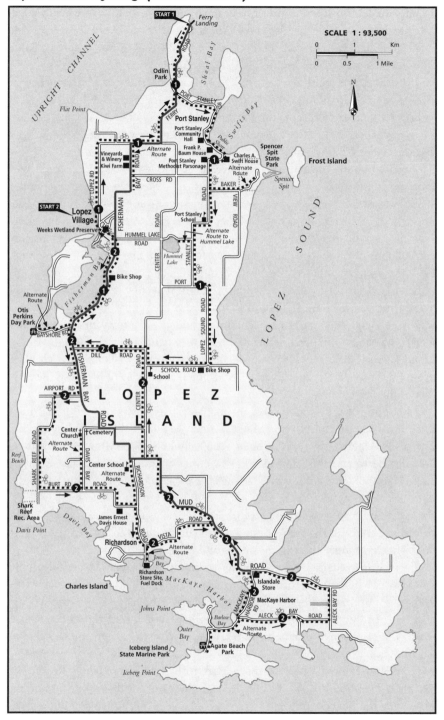

upstairs. Its later history, however, was apparently less than holy, when the hall fell into less reputable hands who ran a brothel here. Several other historic properties in the area include the Charles A. Swift House, Frank P. Baum House, and Port Stanley Methodist Parsonage.

It's a short ride south to the turnoff for Spencer Spit State Park, reached by a 0.5-mile side trip off of Port Stanley Road. The park has about 2 miles of trails and is a particularly pleasant stop for those interested in beachcombing or birding (see chapter 2, hike 17). Spencer Spit is also the only other public park (besides Odlin County Park) that offers camping on Lopez Island.

Heading south on Port Stanley Road, at a jog in the road, you'll pass another of the island's more notable historic structures—the Port Stanley Schoolhouse. The 1917 schoolhouse has undergone some significant changes throughout its history. Closing its doors in 1941 when the island's four school districts consolidated and built today's main school in the middle of the island, the building stood empty and abandoned for almost sixty years. In December 1994 the owners donated the historic building and one acre of land to the Lopez Island Historical Society, with the caveat that it be restored to its condition during its use in the 1920s and 1930s. Today the schoolhouse is used by the historical society and the Lopez community for public meetings, classrooms, social gatherings, and performances. The Lopez School District and the Lopez Island Historical Society also provide an opportunity for island schoolchildren to attend classes here, experiencing a traditional island way of life from the early part of the last century.

Just south of the schoolhouse, a short side trip west along Hummel Lake Road leads to peaceful Hummel Lake, a thirty-six-acre lake fringed by cattails, with a small launching area for boats. You'll find a short trail wandering along the edge between forest and meadow, eventually ending at the lake's floating dock. Hummel Lake is a favorite fishing spot for islanders, one of the few freshwater lakes and ponds on the island. The San Juan County Land Bank has purchased eighty acres around the lake to preserve its wetlands and provide public access, and it's been the subject of an active community restoration effort, with the planting of more than 1,500 shrubs and trees.

Back on Port Stanley Road heading south, the road enters forest and climbs a short hill, where you'll turn left onto Lopez Sound Road, which quickly jogs to the right under a canopy of cool forest. (Unlike the name suggests, there are no views of Lopez Sound from here.) From here, you'll turn right onto School Road, where a short but steep climb takes you past fields and the new Lopez Island School.

To complete the island's northern loop, turn right onto Center Road, then quickly left onto Dill Road. Center Road is the main north-south route on the island, and it's the most traveled by cars—keep an eye out for passing traffic here.

Life preservers at Hummel Lake, Lopez Island

Continuing on the northern loop, after 1.2 miles on Dill Road, you'll turn right (north) onto Fisherman Bay Road, where a quick descent brings you to the shores of Fisherman Bay. For a short, scenic side trip to Otis Perkins Day Park, turn left onto Bayshore Road. This small park and the adjoining beaches and marsh are particularly rich with bird life and are among the best birding spots on Lopez Island.

Back on Fisherman Bay Road, it's a short ride of just under 2 miles to Lopez Village, reached by turning left at the Lopez Island Library just past the intersection with Hummel Lake Road.

Cozy Lopez Village epitomizes the relaxed, peaceful way of life on the island. You'll find several historic properties here, including the Lopez Congregational Church, in continuous use since it was constructed in 1904. Or visit the Weeks Family Water Towers, built between 1914 and 1916 by one of the first families to homestead the area in the 1850s. Water was pumped from wells by a gasoline engine up to the towers, where gravity would carry the water down for use on surrounding farms.

The Lopez Island Farmers Market is open on Saturdays in Lopez Village from June through September. You'll find Lopez Island–grown produce and crafts from local artists including salad greens, vegetables, flowers, and fruit in season, along with jams, chutney, cooking oils, and other items. Local residents also sell a wide variety of arts and crafts items, furniture, metal works, and other products.

Another worthwhile stop in Lopez Village is the Lopez Historical Museum (360–468–2049). The museum, which collects and preserves the regional history of Lopez and the San Juan Islands, features artifacts reflecting Lopez Island's contributions to the maritime, fishing, and farming industries. An extensive archive of documents and artifacts depicts late 1800s and early 1900s Lopez life. The museum is open noon to 4:00 P.M. Friday through Sunday in May and September. In June, July, and August it's open from noon to 4:00 P.M., Wednesday through Sunday.

Just west of Lopez Village at the end of Weeks Point Way is the twenty-two-acre Weeks Wetland Preserve, supporting a rich abundance of wildlife around a saltwater marsh near the mouth of Fisherman Bay. A short interpretive trail meanders through the wetland, ending at an observation deck overlooking the marsh. The tidal flats and mosaic of distinct wetland plant communities provide vital habitat for many species of migrating birds including great blue herons, bald eagles, yellowlegs, snipe, western sandpipers, black-bellied plovers, dowitchers, and several types of swallows. Osprey can often be seen hovering over the shallows before plunging sharply into the water to catch fish. The wetland also provides habitat for river otters, frogs, and salamanders.

Once you've finished exploring Lopez Village, cycle north along Lopez Road, a quieter alternative to Fisherman Bay Road. In 1.7 miles and after a sharp turn to the right, you'll reach the intersection with Fisherman Bay Road. From here, you'll turn left to reach the ferry, but a good side diversion can be found by turning right onto Fisherman Bay Road, where after a short pedal you'll find Lopez Island Vineyards' six-acre organic vineyard and winery (360–468–3644, www.lopezislandvineyards.com). The vineyard grows grapes from northern Europe and sells other wines from grapes from the Yakima Valley. Right next to Lopez Island Vineyards is Lopez Kiwi (360–468–3243), which grows kiwis for delivery to markets in January, along with apples, pears, and raspberries available in fall.

Continuing north on Ferry Road toward the ferry landing, you'll find the Stella Flora Farm (360–468–4181), a family-run farm dedicated to organic and biodynamic agriculture. The owners offer seasonal heirloom produce, potted roses and plants, cut flowers, culinary and medicinal herbs, and a variety of apples. Look for the roadside board to see what's being offered at the site. From here, it's just a short ride back to the ferry landing.

2 South End of Lopez Island

See map on page 145

WHAT TO EXPECT: Cycle past Shark Reef, the historic Richardson Village site, and Agate Beach, experiencing the rolling farmland, rich history, and rugged coast of the south half of Lopez Island.

APPROXIMATE LENGTH: 18 miles

DIFFICULTY: Moderate due to intermediate length and some rolling hills

The Ride

Perhaps more than anyplace else on the main islands of the San Juan archipelago, the south end of Lopez Island feels far removed and perhaps a few steps back in time from the buzz of the nearby mainland cities. Over forty-five farms on Lopez Island derive income from a variety of goods, from fruit to livestock, many of them spread out over the 100-foot-high plateau on the south end of the island. Except for one small store, you'll find a quiet rural life here.

This loop starts from Lopez Village and heads south, allowing for stops at Shark Reef Recreation Area, the historic Richardson town site, and scenic Agate Beach. After a 1.6-mile cycle along Fisherman Bay, you'll climb moderately away from the bay for 0.5 mile, continuing south on Fisherman Bay Road. Approximately 0.8 mile past the intersection with Dill Road, turn right (west) onto Airport Road, then left (south) onto Shark Reef Road after another 0.4 mile. After 1.7 miles of riding through pleasant forest, you'll reach a small parking area and bike rack for Shark Reef, reached by a ten-minute hike through forest.

From Shark Reef Road, turn left (east) onto Burt Road, a very scenic stretch of unstriped rural road that rolls for 2.5 miles past several small farms. An interesting 1-mile side trip on Davis Bay Road will take you past Center Church, constructed between 1887 and 1889, and the adjacent 1884 Union Cemetery. Built by volunteer labor, the church has been in continuous use for church services, weddings, funerals, and social gatherings for several denominations.

Along Davis Bay Road you'll pass the 1913–1914 James Ernest Davis house, one of the few large, elegant farmhouses still standing on Lopez. Davis's parents came to the island in 1869, importing cattle from Texas and selling meat to the English Camp on San Juan Island.

At Richardson Road, you'll turn right (south) toward the town of Richardson. For a small side trip, you can first turn left (north) onto Richardson Road and cycle less than a mile to visit the historic Center School. Built as a two-room schoolhouse, the original structure included a bell tower mounted over the porch. In the 1940s the Lopez Grange acquired the building, where the farming community continues to hold monthly meetings.

Cycling near Richardson, Lopez Island

Turning right onto Richardson Road from Davis Bay Road, after 0.7 mile you'll reach a small side road that turns right (south) to the town of Richardson. The historic town site, now little more than a few homes clustered around a fueling dock, dates back to 1874, when it was the hub of the south end of Lopez. With the tranquility you'll find here today, it's hard to imagine that the historic village was once a bustling port for cargo steamers and fishing boats, home to the Lundy general store and oil tanks for passing boats. The general store stocked everything from oxen yokes to ice cream cones, and its owner proudly boasted, "If you can't find it, you don't need it." In 1985 the store was added to the National Register of Historic Places, but sadly it burned down only five years later. A large salmon cannery located west of the store operated from 1913 to 1921, supporting the region's vibrant salmon-fishing industry.

Richardson Road swings left (east) and becomes Vista Road, joining Mud Bay Road after 1.2 miles. In another mile you'll reach the junction of Mud Bay Road and MacKaye Harbor Road, where you'll turn right (south). The road descends a short hill, closely following the shores of placid MacKaye Harbor. Here, turn left (east) onto Aleck Bay Road, but not before considering the short 0.9-mile side trip to Agate Beach, where you'll find public beach access, a picnic table, and an outhouse. From here, you can also get a good overview of the rugged south shore of the island, with views across Outer Bay to the channel marker on Iceberg Point.

Back on Aleck Bay Road, you'll head east for 2 miles, where after a sharp turn to the left, you'll once again reach Mud Bay Road. To finish the southern loop, turn left here and bike north on Mud Bay Road for 4.2 miles, then turn left and then quickly right onto Center Road. After 1.7 miles turn left onto Dill Road, then quickly right onto Fisherman Bay Road, descending back to Fisherman Bay and Lopez Village.

For More Information

Lopez Bicycle Works (2847 Fisherman Bay Road, 360–468–2847, www.lopez bicycleworks.com) offers road- and mountain-bike rentals and repairs, and sells bikes, parts, and accessories.

San Juan Island

Being the largest and arguably the most diverse of the San Juan Islands, San Juan Island offers cyclists a little bit of everything, from a historic harbor town to farms, forests, quiet bays, and sweeping ocean views. A complete circumnavigation of the island is more than 40 miles, and you'll find more hills than on Lopez, although most hill climbs are moderate in both length and grade. Because it's the most populated, there also tends to be more traffic on San Juan Island, particularly on Roche Harbor Road, which connects Friday Harbor and Roche Harbor. While sections of the busier roads—Cattle Point, Roche Harbor, and Beaverton Valley Roads—thankfully have shoulders, like the other islands many of the smaller roads do not, but traffic volumes are low. Like Lopez, many quiet side roads offer opportunities for loop trips of all lengths and many diversions along the way. A series of eight roadside bike turnouts around the island provide some safe resting spots for cyclists.

San Juan Island also has an active farming community, with over forty farms growing a wide array of products. A helpful pamphlet is the *San Juan Island Farm Products Guide* (360–378–4414, http://sanjuan.wsu.edu/pdf/farmguide .pdf), describing both the various farm products grown on the island and the farms that are seasonally open to the public.

3 Turn Point–Pear Point Loop

WHAT TO EXPECT: A short, scenic loop from Friday Harbor along a quiet road, with views of Turn Island, Jackson Beach, and Griffin Bay

APPROXIMATE LENGTH: 6 miles

DIFFICULTY: Easy due to short distance and gentle terrain

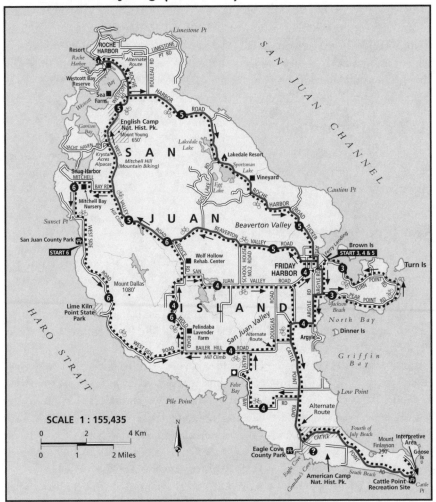

The Ride

This short, easy ride is a quick trip from Friday Harbor, with fairly light traffic and scenery along the way. If you're staying in town, it's a good opportunity to stretch your legs, or you can combine it with longer trips on the island.

Begin your trip by cycling south out of Friday Harbor on Argyle Road, passing the County Fair Grounds, descending a hill, and turning left onto Pear Point Road. About 0.5 mile from the turnoff, you'll pass a right turnoff to Jackson Beach, a long driftwood-covered beach that's also a popular launching spot for kayakers exploring Griffin Bay (see chapter 3, kayak trip 5).

Continuing on the main road (Pear Point), the surface becomes gravel immediately past the Jackson Beach turnoff. Gravel is deep in places, and

San Juan Historical Museum

While you're in Friday Harbor, check out the San Juan Historical Museum (360–378–3949, www.sjmuseum.org), boasting to be the northwestern-most museum in the United States! The museum's collection shares and interprets the story of the people of San Juan Island. The buildings include a log cabin, old jail, milk house, and residence, along with photographs and archival documents.

cyclists should cross this section with care. Pavement resumes after the road quickly passes a sand-and-gravel operation (the least scenic part of the ride). From here you'll find nice water views with a few small hills. Halfway around the point the road changes names, becoming Turn Point Road. At the small beach access point here, you get good views across the narrow channel separating San Juan Island from Turn Island State Marine Park just offshore.

As you approach Friday Harbor again, you'll pass a few residences, along with several marinas and boatyards along Shipyard Harbor before descending back to the ferry landing in Friday Harbor.

4 Cattle Point–False Bay–San Juan Valley Loop

See map on page 152

WHAT TO EXPECT: A tour of the valley farms and shoreline along the south half of San Juan Island

APPROXIMATE LENGTH: 12 miles (25 miles with side trip to Cattle Point)

DIFFICULTY: Moderate due to intermediate length (more difficult with side trip to Cattle Point)

The Ride

This moderate trip tours the south half of San Juan Island, with its valley farms, sweeping south coastline, and quiet roads. The loop actually offers the option of a shorter trip of 12 miles, or a longer ride that takes in American Camp and Cattle Point on the south tip of the island. You can easily combine this ride with several hikes of varying lengths in American Camp.

To begin your trip, you'll cycle south from Friday Harbor on Argyle Road until it becomes Cattle Point Road. As you head south, you'll pass Jackson Beach, with scenic views out over Griffin Bay. About 1.8 miles from town,

False Bay, San Juan Island

Cattle Point Road jogs to the right and then left, passing several bed-and-breakfasts along the way.

About 4 miles south of town, you'll turn off Cattle Point Road onto False Bay Road. On the way you'll pass one of San Juan Island's many farms, the Z Lazy J, that sells goods and produce to the public. The farm seasonally sells cut flowers, produce, preserves, and handcrafted items at a self-serve farm stand.

As another option that can add up to 13 miles (out and back) to your trip, you can continue south on Cattle Point Road. Approximately 3 miles past the False Bay turnoff, Cattle Point Road curves to the left, and you'll reach Eagle Cove County Park (with shoreline access), then shortly after, the visitor center at American Camp, part of San Juan Island National Historical Park. You can easily spend several hours hiking at American Camp, with several hike options of varying lengths and difficulties (see chapter 2, hikes 7, 8, and 9). From here, it's another 3 very scenic miles of cycling to the Cattle Point Lighthouse, where you'll find another hike, with sweeping prairie and ocean views along your ride.

If you opt for the shorter loop, False Bay Road is flat to slightly downhill with very light traffic and abundant scenery. After about 2 miles the road becomes dirt as it winds around False Bay, a marine preserve that has some of the most extensive mudflats at low tide in the San Juan Islands. The mudflats provide some of the best shorebird habitat in the San Juans—nearly every species that's ever been recorded in the islands has been observed here. You'll spot black-bellied plovers, killdeers, and dunlins foraging in the mudflats, and it's a good place to see the many different types of gulls and sandpipers inhabiting the islands.

False Bay Road connects to Bailer Hill Road after 3.5 more miles of cycling along a flat, quiet road through farmland. At this intersection, you'll turn left and follow Bailer Hill Road up a moderate hill climb to Wold Road. For a shorter trip option, turn right from False Bay Road onto Bailer Hill Road. Bailer Hill will turn to the left and become Douglas Road. Here, turn quickly right onto Little Road, then left onto Cattle Point Road, retracing your route north back to Friday Harbor.

Just 0.6 mile north on Wold Road is the Pelindaba Lavender Farm (866–819–1911, www.pelindaba.com), one of the many vibrant organic farms on the island. The owners of the twenty-acre farm welcome guests—you can relax in the gardens or take a guided or self-guided tour of the 10,000 lavender plants in its fields or of the distillery from spring through the end of August. The small store offers lots of inventive products, from lavender peppers and vinegar to soaps and lotions. There's even a lavender festival held here on the second weekend of July.

Continuing north on Wold Road, you'll turn right onto San Juan Valley Road, which eventually turns into Spring Street, and in approximately 4 miles will lead you back to Friday Harbor.

5 Friday Harbor–Beaverton Valley–Roche Harbor

See map on page 152

WHAT TO EXPECT: A moderate loop along the north half of San Juan Island, through the scenic farmland of the Beaverton Valley and past historic English Camp and Roche Harbor

APPROXIMATE LENGTH: 25 miles

DIFFICULTY: More difficult due to length and moderate hill climbs

The Ride

This moderate loop from Friday Harbor gives you a good overview of the north half of San Juan Island. Crossing through the fertile center of the island, you'll have opportunities to stop at farms along the way, take short walks in English Camp, tour Roche Harbor and an interesting sculpture park, and even do a bit of wine tasting. And while this route is also among the most heavily traveled by cars on the island, shoulders on both Beaverton Valley and Roche Harbor Roads help make the cycling experience safer and more enjoyable.

From Friday Harbor, you'll start by cycling west on Second Street, which eventually turns into Guard Street, and finally Beaverton Valley Road. While the loop can be traveled in the opposite direction, it's best to cycle this loop by pedaling west on Beaverton Valley Road to avoid a steep hill climb, returning by way of Roche Harbor Road.

The first leg of the trip along Beaverton Valley Road is a fairly gentle ride through the rural landscape that is quickly reached outside of Friday Harbor. In total, you'll ride about 4.5 miles from Friday Harbor to the intersection with Boyce Road, after which Beaverton Valley Road turns into West Valley Road.

You'll find the hilliest part of this ride along the 2.4 miles on West Valley Road between Boyce Road and Mitchell Bay Road. A moderate climb of 150 vertical feet over 1.4 miles starting after the intersection with Boyce Road leads to a breezy descent of 300 vertical feet over the next mile to the intersection with Mitchell Bay Road. Ride this section of road with caution, as the road's shoulder disappears as you start to climb, and there is no shoulder on the downhill descent.

From the intersection with Mitchell Bay Road, it's 0.9 mile of cycling north on West Valley Road to Krystal Acres Alpacas (360–378–2596, www.krystal acres.com), a farm raising these shy and intelligent creatures, cousins of the llama, that are imported from South America and prized for their soft wool. You're free to wander the farm, and you'll find a small store that sells clothing and gifts.

Just a short 0.5 mile of riding north on West Valley Road will bring you to the entrance for the English Camp unit of San Juan Island National Historical Park. Here, you can spend a few hours enjoying three short hikes, including a walk to Bell Point and around the historic parade grounds, as well as a climb of 1 mile to the scenic views from the summit of Mount Young (see chapter 2, hike 12).

Continuing north from English Camp, you'll soon arrive at the intersection with Roche Harbor Road. Turning right here will take you back to Friday Harbor in approximately 9 miles, and 3-foot-wide shoulders along the entire length of the road make cycling alongside traffic relatively safe. However, the 0.9-mile trip to Roche Harbor, reached by cycling north on Roche Harbor Road, is well worth the side trip.

About 0.4 mile after the intersection with West Valley Road, you'll find on your left a turnoff, which in another 0.8 mile will take you to Westcott Bay Sea Farms (360–378–2489, www.westcottbay.com), which grows oysters on the shores of Westcott Bay. Visitors can purchase live oysters and clams here by the pound, or you're welcome to harvest your own.

Westcott Bay sculpture park, San Juan Island

Just before reaching Roche Harbor, you'll pass the Westcott Bay Reserve (360–370–5050, www.wbay.org), a symbol of the lively arts community in the San Juans. The nineteen-acre outdoor sculpture park, set around a small pond amid rolling fields and forest, has more than one hundred different works from a variety of local artists, ranging from sublime to wild. Trails wind among the sculptures and down to the shoreline of Westcott Bay. Plans are also under way for a learning center at the site.

Just past the sculpture park is the entrance to Roche Harbor. Once the largest lime company west of the Mississippi River in the late 1800s and early 1900s, the present-day resort spreads across several acres and is a mixture of historic charm and opulence. With a grocery store, bar, and fine dining room, it's a good place to grab some food, enjoy the gardens, or gawk at some of the enormous boats in the resort's marina. Several structures in the village are on the National Register of Historic Places, including the 1886 Hotel de Haro, company town cottages, the chapel, a mausoleum, the cemetery, lime quarries, and kiln batteries.

The ride east back to Friday Harbor along Roche Harbor Road is largely forested with gently hilly terrain. Along the way you'll pass Lakedale Resort, the largest spot on the island for camping (including camps set aside for

Mountain Biking San Juan Island

While most of the biking you'll find on San Juan Island is on its paved roads, mountain bikers might want to pay a visit to Mitchell Hill, the Department of Natural Resources land located southeast of English Camp. While not overly technical, the area contains several old logging roads that do require knobby tires and the occasional low gear for some good hill climbs. The network of trails here, however, can be confusing and trails are not maintained. For more information and trail maps, see the San Juan Island Trails Committee Web site (www.sanjuanislandtrails.org).

cyclists), and soon after, Sportsman Lake, just east of the intersection with Egg Lake Road. The lake is popular for fishing and birding. Keep an eye out for common and barrow's goldeneye here, along with gulls, ospreys, and swallows.

Just east of Sportsman Lake along Roche Harbor Road are the thirty-four acres of the San Juan Vineyards (360–378–WINE, www.sanjuanvineyards .com), where you can stop for a taste of their chardonnay, Riesling, merlot, and syrah in their tasting room, housed in a converted historic schoolhouse.

From here, it's just another 3.2 miles east along Roche Harbor Road, through gentle open terrain, back to Friday Harbor. Roche Harbor Road will turn into Tucker Avenue, and at the intersection with Guard Street, turn left to reach the center of town.

6 West Side Road–West Valley Road Loop

See map on page 152

WHAT TO EXPECT: A moderately hilly loop trip from San Juan County Park that encompasses sweeping views over Haro Strait

APPROXIMATE LENGTH: 16.5 miles

DIFFICULTY: More difficult due to length and moderate hill climbs

The Ride

If you've come to San Juan Island to experience its famous views over Haro Strait and to spot whales, this is the ride for you. This moderate loop is a particularly good option for those wanting to start their ride from one of the parks on the west side of the island—stronger cyclists might combine it with other loop rides on the island. To avoid the largest hill climbs on West Side Road, it's best to ride this loop by cycling south on this road.

The route starts at San Juan County Park, where you'll turn right (south) onto West Side Road, immediately climbing through cool forest, passing a small pond and the San Juan County Land Bank day-use area at 1.7 miles. From here, following a quick descent and hairpin turn, views over Haro Strait will open up before you just after reaching Lime Kiln Point State Park. The park, famous as the best spot on San Juan Island to watch orca whales, also has a historic lighthouse and a 1-mile trail leading along the shoreline and past historic lime kilns (see chapter 2, hike 11).

Continuing south on West Side Road, the views are magnificent. California poppies brighten the hillsides along the road with vibrant orange in the spring. The San Juan County Land Bank has thankfully purchased over 4,000 feet of shoreline along this road, protecting the spectacular views here and providing access to the shoreline. If you're here in the evening, it's also a great place to catch the sunset.

Approximately 2.3 miles past Lime Kiln State Park, the road turns away from the shoreline and becomes Bailer Hill Road. Turn left onto Wold Road, which passes through scenic farmland and past the Pelindaba Lavender Farm (866–819–1911, www.pelindaba.com), which is open to the public. In 1.9 miles

Open meadows along West Side Road, San Juan Island

from Bailer Hill Road, you'll reach an intersection with San Juan Valley Road and Boyce Road. Continue straight ahead (north) on Boyce Road, which will reach West Valley Road/Beaverton Road in less than a mile. Along Boyce Road you'll pass the Wolf Hollow Rehabilitation Center (not open to the public), providing animal rescue and rehabilitation for a wide variety of injured animals from throughout Washington.

Turn left onto West Valley Road, where you'll find a moderate climb over the next 1.4 miles, followed by a steep descent for a mile (descend with caution, no road shoulder here), where you'll turn left onto Mitchell Bay Road. Along this road you'll find Mitchell Bay Farms and Nursery (360–378–2309), selling lamb, fruits, berries, and nursery stock. The farm is open seasonally to the public Thursday through Saturday from 10:00 A.M. to 3:00 P.M.

At the next junction, turn left onto West Side Road, which after 1.9 miles of rolling terrain will bring you back to your starting point at San Juan County Park.

For More Information

Island Bicycles, San Juan Island, (360) 378–4941, www.islandbicycles.com

Orcas Island

As the most rugged of the main islands in the San Juans, Orcas Island offers a different experience for cyclists in contrast to Lopez and San Juan Islands. Here, you'll find longer and steeper hill climbs, along with fewer opportunities for loop trips. At the same time, Orcas offers the only real mountain biking in the main islands, along with the challenge of climbing the grueling Mount Constitution Road to the summit, then rewarding yourself with the exhilarating ride back down. If you're coming to mountain bike, it's a good idea to check ahead of time with staff at Moran State Park regarding the latest trail-use regulations, as they're subject to change.

7 Orcas Landing–Crow Valley–East Sound

WHAT TO EXPECT: A moderate ride through a pastoral valley and past historic villages to Orcas Island's center, with several side trips along the way

APPROXIMATE LENGTH: 9.5 miles one-way to East Sound, plus side trips

DIFFICULTY: Moderate due to modest length and hill climbs

Orcas Island Cycling (Rides 7–9)

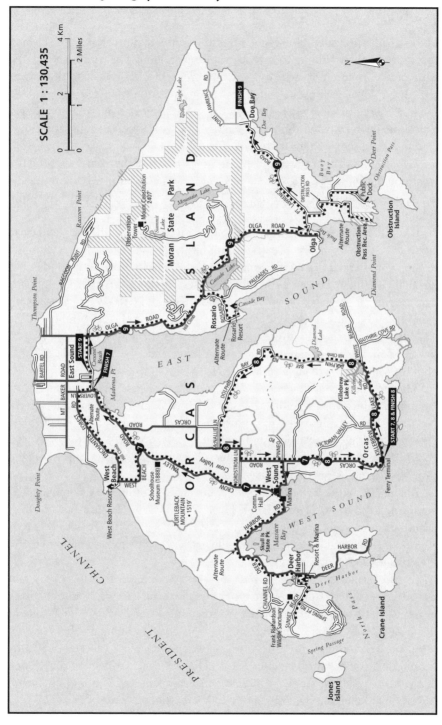

The Ride

Orcas Road (also called Horseshoe Highway) is the main road on Orcas Island that links the ferry landing to the village of East Sound. The route can be busy, particularly around ferry arrival times, and cyclists will find little in the way of a road shoulder, making the traffic feel at times a little too close for comfort. Luckily, there are some alternative routes to East Sound that will not only get you off major sections of this road, but also give you a look at some of the quieter and more scenic sides of Orcas Island.

Starting from either the ferry landing or East Sound, this route is among the most popular on the island, due to its scenic farms and historic buildings, gentler terrain compared to other parts of the island, and the relatively low traffic volumes.

If you're riding from the ferry landing, you'll turn left off the ferry and cycle north on Orcas Road. Cycling past small farms and through moderately hilly terrain, you'll reach the intersection with Deer Harbor Road in 2.6 miles and turn left. You'll quickly reach the village of West Sound, a small cluster of buildings around the intersection of Deer Harbor Road and Crow Valley Road, with a marina and county dock, a historic community hall, and a restaurant.

You have the option here of turning right (north) onto Crow Valley Road toward East Sound, or continuing straight ahead for the scenic ride to Deer Harbor, which will add about 6 miles (out and back) to your trip.

The ride between West Sound and Deer Harbor passes along scenic Massacre Bay, named for the Indian massacre that took place here in 1858. Fierce Northern Indians ambushed the tranquil Lummi Indians on the beach here, reportedly killing more than one hundred in the process. Sour history aside, you'll get scenic views out over the bay through juniper and oak woodland along this 1-mile stretch of road.

About 1.6 miles from West Sound, the road climbs away from the bay before descending to Deer Harbor. Deer Harbor is the former site of Orcas Island's only fish cannery and one of the oldest villages in the islands. Today it's a bustling port, with a marina, a dockside grocery store, historic buildings, and the upscale Deer Harbor resort.

Before retracing your route back to West Sound, bird enthusiasts might consider the short 1-mile side trip (with a short but steep hill climb) to the Frank Richardson Wildlife Sanctuary, protecting Deer Harbor Marsh, one of the most extensive freshwater wetlands in the islands. Heading north away from Deer Harbor and back toward West Sound, the sanctuary can be reached by turning left (west) onto Channel Road. The sanctuary, which can be viewed from the roadside, is home to grebes, mallards, blue-winged and cinnamon teals, hooded mergansers, rails, coots, and several other bird species.

Rural road in Crow Valley, Orcas Island

Once returning to West Sound, you'll turn left (north) and follow Crow Valley Road. For a taste of Orcas history, take a quick stop at the Crow Valley Schoolhouse Museum, a one-room schoolhouse that operated from 1888 to 1918 and is now on the National Register of Historic Places. The school is open in summers by appointment and contains original desks along with a stove, blackboard, teacher's chair, and books.

The total trip from West Sound to the intersection with West Beach Road is approximately 4.75 miles. Here, you can continue straight ahead—Crow Valley Road will quickly join Horseshoe Highway and lead into East Sound in 1.5 miles.

As yet another option, turn left onto West Beach Road, passing small farms and a cemetery, reaching the intersection with Enchanted Forest Road in 1.3 miles. Turn left here to reach the road's end—the rocky beach here is public, while just north of the beach is West Beach Resort (877–WEST–BCH, www.westbeachresort.com), which offers the only camping on the west side of Orcas Island, along with cabins, a small grocery store, and moorage.

While the ride from West Beach east along Enchanted Forest Road to East Sound is only 2.6 miles, you'll contend with a hill climb of 250 feet over a mile with a maximum grade of about 9 percent, followed by a breezy descent to East Sound.

However you get to East Sound, you'll also find plenty of shops and restaurants in town to keep you occupied. The Orcas Island Historical Museum (360–376–4849, www.orcasisland.org/~history) is worth a stop, consisting of six log cabins built by homesteaders between the 1870s and 1890s. You'll find exhibits on early aspects of island life, tools, early island stores, Orcas Island's once-thriving apple industry, homesteading, and Coast Salish Native American life (open mid-May through September). Madrona Point, a scenic park overlooking the water, is reached by a short trail on the south side of Crescent Beach Road.

8 Dolphin Bay Road Loop

See map on page 161

WHAT TO EXPECT: A rugged loop over paved and dirt road with a steep hill climb, exploring the least developed section of Orcas Island outside of Moran State Park

APPROXIMATE LENGTH: 14 miles

DIFFICULTY: More difficult due to steep hill climb and rough road surface

The Ride

This vigorous ride will take you to a wilder corner of Orcas Island by following Dolphin Bay Road, one of the least traveled routes on the island. The middle section of Dolphin Bay Road is gravel, and while theoretically passable by road bikes, the road surface along with the very steep climb makes a mountain bike a much better option for this ride. If you're planning to leave your car around Orcas Landing, be aware that parking is limited and can be difficult to find, particularly on busy summer weekends. If the ferry landing lot is full, you'll have to park along Orcas Road (Horseshoe Highway) once you've climbed the hill away from the ferry landing.

This cycling route starts from the ferry landing, where you'll turn right (east) onto Killebrew Lake Road, climbing past farms and reaching the shallow, lily-pad covered Killebrew Lake in 2.75 miles. Just after the lake, you'll bear left (north) onto Dolphin Bay Road, where pavement quickly ends for the next 4 miles.

The next few miles of the ride cross this quiet, undeveloped side of Orcas Island under the canopy of a cool forest. About 0.5 mile after Killebrew Lake, you'll encounter your steepest climb of the ride, a grind that gains 200 feet with a grade of up to 15 percent. About 1.2 miles from Killebrew Lake, you'll pass quiet Diamond (formerly Martin) Lake, with no facilities but certainly a scenic view and a good opportunity to rest. Just after the lake, a descent of over 300

Cycling past a freshwater lake, Orcas Island

feet over the next mile will make for a fun reward for your climbing. Use caution here as the road surface is dirt and rough in spots. Good brakes are a must.

Reaching pavement again 4 miles from Killebrew Lake, you'll reach in another mile a three-way stop. Continue straight ahead, as Dolphin Bay Road turns into McNallie Lane. Turn left onto Orcas Road (Horseshoe Highway) and follow it south for 4.4 miles back to your starting point.

9 East Sound–Doe Bay

See map on page 161

WHAT TO EXPECT: A mostly moderate ride with one large hill climb along the east shore of East Sound, past lakes and forests in Moran State Park, and through the rural landscape on the east side of Orcas Island

APPROXIMATE LENGTH: 11 miles

DIFFICULTY: Moderate to more difficult due to rolling, moderate hills, punctuated by a big hill climb to the north entrance of Moran State Park

The Ride

This route follows the main road connecting East Sound to the east side of Orcas Island. Because of the island's rugged topography, there's no option for a

Maidenhair fern

loop trip here, but several side diversions will keep your interest along this route.

From East Sound, follow Crescent Beach Road east to the junction with Olga Road and turn right. From here, you'll ride about 3.3 miles to the entrance of Moran State Park. You'll cycle through a patchwork of fields and forests, with occasional views through the trees out to East Sound. The largest hill will challenge cyclists about 1.5 miles south of town, with a climb of about 340 feet over 1.8 miles before reaching the entrance to the park.

For an interesting side trip just before the park entrance, turn right at the ROSARIO RESORT sign and descend the steep road for 1.5 miles (losing 450 feet of elevation in the process—not an easy ride back!) to visit this scenic and historic resort (888–FOR–ROCK, http://rosario.rockresorts.com). You'll find here a marina along with the original mansion built by Robert Moran, whose donation of land helped create Moran State Park. Now serving as a hotel, the 6,000-square-foot Rosario Mansion is listed on the National Register of Historic Places.

Back on Olga Road cycling east, from the park entrance you'll soon pass the North End Campground and reach the shores of placid Cascade Lake, a tempting spot for a swim or picnic during warm weather. Moran State Park also offers a good camping option for cyclists, particularly those who want to explore other parts of the park along its 30 miles of trails, or take on the challenge of cycling the road to the summit of Mount Constitution. Advanced reservations for campsites are highly recommended during the summer.

The road veers away from Cascade Lake, climbing a robust 250 feet to the junction with Mount Constitution Road. From the park's north entrance, you'll descend 600 feet over 2.5 miles on Olga Road (Horseshoe Highway) to the intersection with Point Lawrence Road and the picturesque village of Olga. You'll turn left here onto Point Lawrence Road to continue on to Doe Bay, but the village of Olga, reached by the short trip straight ahead to the end of Olga Road, is a tempting stop with a post office, store, and public dock, along with a cafe and art gallery.

Once on Point Lawrence Road cycling east toward Doe Bay, you'll pass the scenic shores overlooking the mudflats of Buck Bay. Just beyond the bay, another option is the 4.4-mile out-and-back trip to Obstruction Pass, accessible

Mount Constitution Road

No biking chapter about Orcas Island would be complete without mention of the grueling 5-mile climb up the Mount Constitution Road to its summit. Originally built as a wagon road from East Sound, today's paved road, climbing a total elevation of 2,000 feet in a series of switchbacks with grades of up to 15 percent, can be quite a workout, but the views are well worth the effort if driving to the summit just doesn't seem right. (Imagine horses and buggies going up this road.) On the way you'll cycle through beautiful forests, catch several views out over the San Juan Islands, pass quiet ponds and marshes, and be rewarded with knowing that you've made it to the summit on your own power. The ride down is nothing short of exhilarating, although an extra check of your brakes is highly advised.

by bearing right from Point Lawrence Road onto Obstruction Pass Road. After 1 mile and a short hill climb, bear right at a Y in the road and descend an unpaved gravel road to the trailhead for Obstruction Pass Recreation Area, where you'll find a short 0.5-mile trail to a scenic pebble beach (see chapter 2, hike 6). Or, by going left at the Y, you'll reach the public dock at Obstruction Pass, with a view across to Obstruction Island.

Once back on Point Lawrence Road, 3 more miles of moderately hilly riding past small farms and forest will bring you to Doe Bay. Cyclists will find campsites, along with hot tubs and a small store here. Point Lawrence Road continues another 2 miles after Doe Bay, past homes and forests, where it ends at the Sea Acres development.

10 Mount Constitution Summit– Cascade Lake (Mountain Bike)

WHAT TO EXPECT: A scenic descent from the summit of Mount Constitution along open ridges, through beautiful forests, and past scenic lakes in Moran State Park.

APPROXIMATE LENGTH: 10 miles

DIFFICULTY: Moderate due to moderate descent and generally well-graded trail surface

The Ride

While Moran State Park is better known for its hiking, the park's mountain-biking trails also entice campers and day-trippers from the mainland to try out its variety of fire roads and single-track trails. The park has 11 miles of roads and trails open to mountain biking year-round, and it opens an additional 14 miles to mountain bikers from September 15 to May 15, when there are fewer hikers, and fewer chances of conflicts or accidents between the two groups. Check with park staff to get the latest updates regarding not only trail-use rules but also conditions, as blowdowns from windstorms occasionally block the park's trails. While the park's trails are not considered overly technical, you'll find them fairly uncrowded, particularly in the off-season.

Perhaps the most popular mountain bike ride in the park starts from the summit, taking advantage of gravity to descend its way around the mountain and back to Cascade Lake. Due to seasonal closures of some of the park's trails to mountain bikes, this trip can only be done from September 15 to May 15. If you're looking for a workout to start your trip, climb the 5 miles up the paved

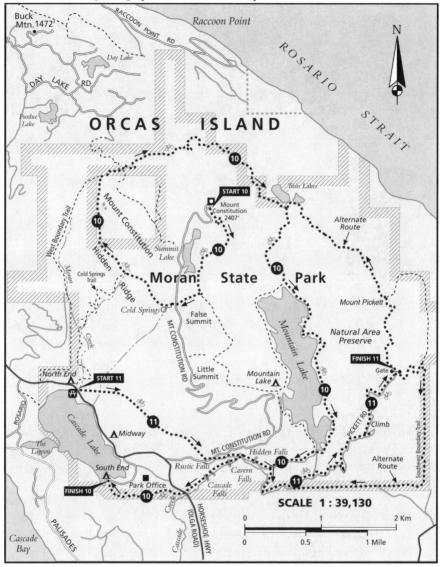

road to the summit (Mount Constitution Road)—otherwise, simply catch a ride to the top.

This ride offers a little bit for everyone, with a combination of single track, fire road, and small sections of paved road, along with some exhilarating steep drops and moderate climbs. You'll also get good views from the summit ridge and bike past some of the park's sparkling lakes and streams along the way.

Cyclists at Moran State Park, Orcas Island

The ride starts on the Ridgetop Trail at the summit parking lot, beginning behind the restroom building, and descends about 350 feet for the first 0.5 mile, with a generally smooth trail surface, moderate grades, and open views. Over the next 0.5 mile, you'll gain back your lost elevation and turn right toward Cold Springs, quickly reaching Mount Constitution Road. Cross the road onto the Cold Springs Trail, passing the historic Civilian Conservation Corps–era shelter and Cold Springs itself. You'll pass a few small wetlands, and in another 0.75 mile reach a junction with the Cold Springs Trail. The Cold Springs Trail offers an alternate way back to Cascade Lake by way of a heady descent down twenty-five switchbacks.

Turning right, you'll pick up the North Trail, moderately descending over the next mile to a crossing of the West Boundary Trail under a powerline. You'll then descend 700 more feet through lush forest over the next 2 miles, ignoring an unmarked jeep road crossing the trail, until you reach the next signed trail junction. Turn left at this junction and make a quick descent to a trail to the left, crossing a bridge to Twin Lakes. Bikes are not permitted around the lakes, but the short trails looping around each lake are a scenic break from your ride.

From the Twin Lakes trail junction, you'll continue straight ahead, descending gently along a scenic stream valley to the north shore of Mountain Lake. You'll traverse the east side of Mountain Lake on well-graded trail (the west side of the lake is closed to mountain biking). At the south end of the lake, just before the dam, you'll find the Cascade Creek Trail descending along Cascade

Creek. As an alternate route, just across the dam a short trail designated for bikes quickly leads to the Mountain Lake Campground.

The trail along Cascade Creek plunges down through lush forest, with a few steep switchbacks to keep an eye out for. At 0.75 mile from Mountain Lake, the trail intersects with Pickett Road; turn right here, the fire road quickly reaching the Cascade Falls trailhead and the Mount Constitution Road. If your final destination is the Cascade Lake picnic area or North End Campground, continue straight ahead on Pickett Road, cross Mount Constitution Road, and pick up the last part of the Cascade Lake Loop Trail, riding it 1.5 miles to its end across from the picnic area.

If you're heading for the South End Campground, turn left onto the Cascade Falls Trail, descending 250 feet past three scenic waterfalls, and crossing Olga Road less than a mile from Pickett Road at a concrete bridge. From here, you can either turn right and ride the paved road, or continue straight ahead to descend to the South End Campground. Either route is less than a mile.

11 Pickett Road–Twin Lakes Loop (Mountain Bike)

See map on page 169

WHAT TO EXPECT: A moderate to steep climb through forest on a double-track fire road, with the option (seasonally) of completing a moderate single-track loop past three lakes and down a scenic stream valley

APPROXIMATE LENGTH: 6 miles out and back to the gate on Pickett Road (open to riding all year); 9-mile loop to Twin Lakes (open seasonally)

DIFFICULTY: Moderate; significant elevation gain but low technical difficulty

The Ride

This route up a double-track fire road, while not technically difficult, includes a good workout that climbs 1,200 feet to a gate near the summit of Mount Pickett. This ride follows lower-elevation trails in Moran State Park, which are among the few trails accessible to mountain bikers year-round. If you're riding in the off-season, you can continue past the gate, descend to Twin Lakes, and then complete a loop back via Mountain Lake and Cascade Creek.

You can start your ride across from the Cascade Lake picnic area, from the South End Campground, or at the Cascade Falls trailhead on the road to the summit of Mount Constitution. Starting from the parking area just across

Big Twin Lake, Orcas Island

the road from the picnic area on Cascade Lake, you'll climb along a forested single-track trail above the lake, quickly reaching a service road above Midway Campground in less than a mile. Turn right onto this road and then quickly left to follow the trail, climbing a short but steep pitch and reaching an intersection with the Cascade Lake Loop Trail.

Here, you'll continue straight ahead and reach Mount Constitution Road. Cross the road to the Cascade Falls trailhead and parking area and continue east from the trailhead on Pickett Road. For those wanting a shorter ride, you can start your trip from this trailhead as well.

From here, the double-track Pickett Road climbs 1,200 feet through beautiful forest to a gate below the forested summit of Mount Pickett (no views here). In the first 0.5 mile, you'll pass single-track side trails along this road, the first descending to Cascade Falls to the right, the second crossing a small footbridge and climbing to Mountain Lake to the left, both pieces of a longer ride you can do seasonally as part of a longer loop past Twin Lakes. At 1.4 miles, stay right at a fork—the left fork quickly leads to the trail around the east side of Mountain Lake.

For the first 2 miles from Mount Constitution Road, you'll gain about 400 feet. The road steepens over the following mile, grinding out another 600 feet in elevation. At 3 miles from Mount Constitution Road, you'll reach an information board and gate. To the right you'll find a trail connecting to the Southeast Boundary Trail, a route following steep switchbacks that are generally not well maintained, with frequent blowdowns across the trail.

From the intersection with the Southeast Boundary Trail, the double-track Pickett Road continues over the Mount Pickett summit and then moderately descends, reaching Twin Lakes after about 2.1 miles. The section of Pickett Road beyond the gate here is only open from September 15 to May 15 to protect an adjacent natural area preserve, so mountain bikers in the peak season will have to settle for either retracing their route back to the Cascade Creek trailhead or cutting over to the Southeast Boundary Trail.

Trails around Twin Lakes are closed to cyclists, but they make a worthwhile short hike for those willing to part with their bikes. At the south end of Twin Lakes, you'll turn left and descend moderately back to the north shore of Mountain Lake. Follow the route along the east side of Mountain Lake. At the south end of the lake, just before the dam, you'll find the Cascade Creek Trail and head back to your starting point.

For More Information

Wildlife Cycles, East Sound, (360) 376–4708, www.wildlifecycles.com

Dolphin Bay Bicycles, Orcas Landing, (360) 376–4157, www.rockisland.com/~dolphin

Marina Bicycle Rentals, Deer Harbor, (360) 376–3037

Other Biking Trails in the Park

Cold Springs Trail: A steep 2.5-mile-long trail with twenty-five switchbacks, the Cold Springs Trail is best ridden down from Cold Springs to Cascade Lake. It offers a shortcut opportunity for those riding down from the summit of Mount Constitution.

West Boundary Trail: The West Boundary Trail climbs 1.25 miles following a powerline from Cascade Lake to its junction with the North Trail. With no switchbacks to ease the grade, it's advisable to ride this one downhill as well. It's arguably the least scenic trail in the park, although it does offer an alternative route down from the summit.

Twin Lakes to Mount Constitution Summit: This trail descends more than 1,400 feet from the summit of Mount Constitution to Twin Lakes via a series of steep switchbacks. It's a brutal climb from Twin Lakes, and it's best to ride this trail from the summit parking lot down to Twin Lakes, offering a shortcut from the summit for those who want a more direct route to Twin Lakes and Mountain Lake.

Shaw Island

The smallest and least developed of the four major islands served by the ferry, Shaw Island makes a bucolic stop for cyclists wanting a fairly quick morning or afternoon ride either as a day trip from the mainland or as a stopover on a longer trip through the San Juans. Ferry service to the island runs from Anacortes daily, or you can simply hop an interisland ferry from one of the other three major islands.

12 Shaw Island Loop

WHAT TO EXPECT: Forest, bay views, historic museum, and schoolhouse
APPROXIMATE DISTANCE: 13 miles
DIFFICULTY: Moderate due to modest hill climbs and distance

The Ride

This 13-mile route from the Shaw Island ferry landing circumnavigates the small island, passing most of the island's public attractions. You'll be biking through forest much of the time, but you'll also wind along bays and past some of the island's small farms.

For those with road bikes, a portion of this loop includes a descent on a fairly rough unpaved road, which can be bypassed by doubling back along the route.

From the ferry landing, follow Blind Bay Road for 1.3 miles to the intersection with Squaw Bay Road at the island's community center. As you cycle along the bay, you'll see tiny Blind Island at the mouth of the bay, where kayakers can stop as part of a day paddle or camp overnight. You'll pass the intersection with Smuggler's Cove Road in another 0.3 mile, then have a long but gradual hill climb that will take you past the Shaw Island Cemetery to the intersection with Ben Nevis Loop Road. Here, take time to explore the island's historical museum (360–468–2637), recognizable by the reef-net fishing boat in front of the building. The museum's collection of old photos, written records, and farming implements document the history of the island. It's open to the public on Tuesday and Saturday afternoons and on Thursday mornings.

At the museum you'll turn right onto Ben Nevis Loop Road, cycling through pleasant forest on a gradual descent. In 2 more miles you'll arrive at the intersection with Neck Point Road. Here, you can turn right for a 4.4-mile out-and-back ride through forest and past homes to the road's end.

Retracing your route back to the intersection of Neck Point Road and Ben Nevis Loop Road, continue straight ahead, reaching again in 1.1 miles the

Shaw Island Cycling (Ride 12)

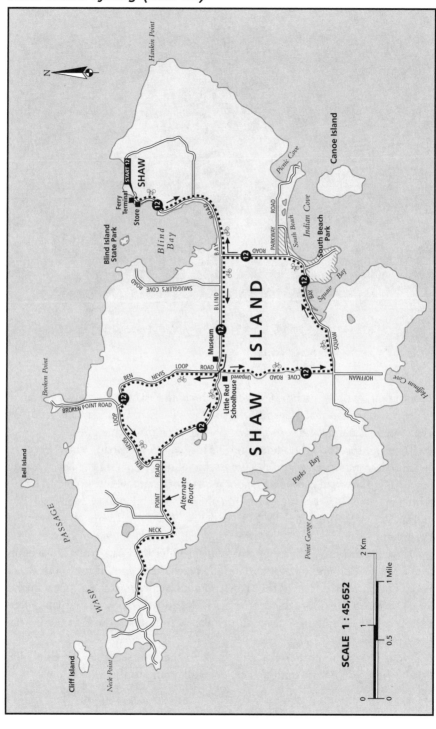

Little Red Schoolhouse, Shaw Island

intersection at the museum. On your right is the island's Little Red School-house, on the National Register of Historic Places, where students from the island are still taught today in grades kindergarten through eighth.

Turn right at the schoolhouse onto Hoffman Cove Road, which becomes dirt and descends steeply for 0.9 mile to the intersection with the paved Squaw Bay Road. (This road is rough in spots and is more suitable for mountain bikes.) Hoffman Cove Road continues straight ahead to its end at the Cedar Rock Biological Preserve, protected in 1975 and now managed by the University of Washington.

Turning left onto Squaw Bay Road, in 1.1 miles the road drops down along scenic Squaw Bay, and in another 0.6 mile reaches the turnoff for South Beach Park. The park, with one of the largest sandy beaches in the San Juans, makes for a good stop to explore the beach, and is the only place on Shaw Island offering overnight camping for drive-in or bike-in campers, as well as for boaters and kayakers.

From here, it's another 0.8 mile back to the intersection with Blind Bay Road, where you'll turn right and retrace your route to the ferry landing.

Research, Conservation, and Education Organizations

Center for Whale Research

Promotes, conducts, and supports research on whales, dolphins, and porpoises.

Friday Harbor, WA 98250

www.rockisland.com/~orcasurv

(360) 378–5835

Friends of the San Juans

Protects the land, water, sea, and livability of the San Juan Islands through science, education, law, and citizen action.

www.sanjuans.org

(360) 378–2319

Lopez Community Land Trust

Acts as a resource for, and to provide access to, permanently affordable housing and land for low-income residents, while cultivating sustainable economic development and nurturing an ethic of land stewardship.

www.lopezclt.org

(360) 468–3723

The Nature Conservancy

Washington State Office

Preserves the plants, animals, and natural communities that represent the diversity of life on Earth by protecting the lands and waters they need to survive. Manages several sites in the San Juan Islands.

http://nature.org/wherewework/northamerica/states/washington/

(206) 343–4344

OPAL Community Land Trust (Orcas Island)

Protects natural resources while also providing homes for people, who are vital to the island's community.

www.opalclt.org

(360) 376–3191

San Juan County Conservation District

Works with landowners and residents to develop sustainable land-use practices that protect and conserve San Juan County's soil and water for habitat, forestry, farming, and other uses.

www.rockisland.com/~sjccd

(360) 378–6621

San Juan County Land Bank

This public program is funded by a real estate transfer tax paid for by purchasers of property in San Juan County. Funds are used to purchase conservation easements and to acquire land outright.

www.co.san-juan.wa.us/land_bank
(360) 378–4402

San Juan Island Trails Committee

Encourages the creation and maintenance of a network of trails for nonmotorized use on San Juan Island.

www.sanjuanislandtrails.org

San Juan Islands National Wildlife Refuge

Includes eighty-three islands in the San Juan archipelago, totaling 454 acres.

www.r1.fws.gov/refuges/field/wa_sanjuanis.htm
(360) 457–8451

San Juan Preservation Trust

Dedicated to helping people protect the wildlife, scenery, and traditional way of life of the San Juan Islands through the preservation and careful use of land.

www.sjpt.org
(360) 468–3202

Books and Other Reading

Adams, Evelyn. 1995. *San Juan Islands Wildlife: A Handbook for Exploring Nature*. The Mountaineers Books, Seattle, WA.

Alt, David and Donald W. Hyndman. 1995. *Northwest Exposures: A Geologic Story of the Northwest*. Mountain Press, Missoula, MT.

Angell, Tony and Kenneth C. Balcomb. 1982. *Marine Birds and Mammals of Puget Sound*. University of Washington Press, Seattle, WA.

Atkinson, S. R. and F. S. Sharpe. 1985. *Wild Plants of the San Juan Islands*. The Mountaineers Books, Seattle, WA.

Bailey, Jo and Carl Nyberg. 2000. *Gunkholing the San Juan Islands*. San Juan Enterprises, Seattle, WA.

Burch, David. 1999. *Fundamentals of Kayak Navigation*. Globe Pequot Press, Guilford, CT.

Dowd, J. 1988. *Sea Kayaking: A Manual for Long Distance Touring* (3rd edition). University of Washington Press, Seattle, WA.

Hutchinson, D. 2004. *The Complete Book of Sea Kayaking* (5th edition). Falcon, Globe Pequot Press, Guilford, CT.

Kozloff, Eugene. 1973. *Seashore Life of Puget Sound, the Strait of Georgia, and the San Juan Archipelago*. University of Washington Press, Seattle, WA.

Lamb, A. and P. Edgell. 1986. *Coastal Fishes of the Pacific Northwest*. Harbour Publishing, Madiera, B.C.

Lewis, M. G. and F. S. Sharpe. 1987. *Birding in the San Juan Islands*. The Mountaineers Books, Seattle, WA.

MacGowan, Craig. 1993. *Mac's Field Guides: San Juans and Gulf Islands*. The Mountaineers Books, Seattle, WA.

Osborne, R. W., J. Calambokidis, and E. Dorsey. 1988. *Marine Mammals of Greater Puget Sound*. Islands Press, Anacortes, WA.

Pratt-Johnson, Betty. 1997. *99 Dives from the San Juan Islands in Washington to the Gulf Islands*. Heritage House Publishing Company, Surrey, B.C.

Stein, Julie K. 2000. *Exploring Coast Salish Prehistory: The Archaeology of San Juan Island*. University of Washington Press, Seattle, WA.

About the Author

Dave Wortman writes about travel, the outdoors, and the environment from his home in Seattle, Washington. An avid hiker, he has written for a variety of publications including *Sierra Magazine, High Country News, Mother Earth News, E Magazine*, the *Seattle Post-Intelligencer*, and the *Portland Oregonian*. He was also the revision author for the second edition of *Hiking Washington* for The Globe Pequot Press.